# FIGHTING WITH THE DESERT RATS

Previously published in 1945 as

*An Infantry Officer With the Eighth Army*

*The Personal Experiences of an Infantry Officer
During the Eighth Army's Campaign Through Africa and Sicily*

# FIGHTING WITH THE DESERT RATS

## AN INFANTRY OFFICER'S WAR WITH THE EIGHTH ARMY

**MAJOR H.P. SAMWELL MC**
Presented by **MARTIN MACE & JOHN GREHAN**

Pen & Sword
**MILITARY**

First published in Great Britain in 1945 by
William Blackwood & Sons Ltd.

Reprinted in this format in 2012 by
Pen & Sword Military
An imprint of
Pen & Sword Books Ltd
47 Church Street
Barnsley
South Yorkshire
S70 2AS

ISBN 978 1 84884 766 8

The Publishers have made every effort to trace the authors,
their estates and their agents without success and they would be interested
to hear from anyone who is able to provide them with this information.

A CIP catalogue record for this book is
available from the British Library

All rights reserved. No part of this book may be reproduced or transmitted in
any form or by any means, electronic or mechanical including photocopying,
recording or by any information storage and retrieval system,
without permission from the Publisher in writing.

Printed and bound in England
By CPI Group (UK) Ltd, Croydon, CR0 4YY

Pen & Sword Books Ltd incorporates the Imprints of Pen & Sword Aviation,
Pen & Sword Family History, Pen & Sword Maritime, Pen & Sword Military,
Pen & Sword Discovery, Wharncliffe Local History, Wharncliffe True Crime,
Wharncliffe Transport, Pen & Sword Select, Pen & Sword Military Classics,
Leo Cooper, The Praetorian Press, Remember When,
Seaforth Publishing and Frontline Publishing

For a complete list of Pen & Sword titles please contact
PEN & SWORD BOOKS LIMITED
47 Church Street, Barnsley, South Yorkshire, S70 2AS, England
E-mail: enquiries@pen-and-sword.co.uk
Website: www.pen-and-sword.co.uk

# LEADING FROM THE FRONT

"It was deathly still and a full moon lighted the bleak sand as if it were day. Suddenly the silence was broken by the crash of a single gun, and the next moment a mighty roar rent the air and the ground shook under us as salvo after salvo crashed out from hundreds of guns." This bombardment marked the opening of the Second Battle of El Alamein. It also marked the beginning of the run of victories by the British Eighth Army that would drive Rommel's famed *Afrika Korps* back across North Africa, leading to the Germans eventual surrender in that theatre of the war in May 1943.

Hugh Peter de Lancy Samwell, a young infantry officer, was a part of that enormously successful campaign which continued across the Straits of Messina and into Italy.

The son of Rev. Edward Hugh Samwell, Rector of Christ Church, Falkirk, and Florence Nellie Kate Samwell, Hugh was born on 8 July 1911, in Stockport, Manchester. Whilst a pupil at Trinity College, Glenalmond (now Glenalmond College), he joined the school's Officer Training Corps, attaining the rank of Cadet Corporal.

On 1 January 1938, Samwell was commissioned as a Second Lieutenant in the 7th Battalion The Argyll and Sutherland Highlanders (Princess Louise's) – a Territorial Army unit. With the outbreak of war imminent, on 24 August 1939, the regiment was mobilized. Continuing to serve with the 7th Battalion The Argyll and Sutherland Highlanders, on 1 January 1941, Samwell was promoted to the rank of War Substantive Lieutenant.

The battalion sailed for Egypt in June 1942 following a period of home defence duties on the south coast of England and north-east coast of Scotland after the Fall of France. Along with its sister unit, the 8th Battalion and the 1st Battalion The Black Watch, the battalion formed the 154th Infantry Brigade, part of the 51st (Highland) Division, one of ten divisions and several independent brigades which comprised the British Eighth Army. By the time of the Battle of El Alamein the Eighth Army numbered some 220,000 men.

The Eighth Army was created in September 1941 out of the Western Desert Force which had faced the full might of the Italian Army that had invaded Egypt in September 1940. The Italians were comprehensively beaten and when the Allies moved onto the offensive, the Italians were driven back into Libya, and eventually the Italian 10th Army surrendered.

The Italians were in danger of losing their entire North African empire and they appealed for help from Germany. The consequence of this was the arrival of General Rommel and the creation of the *Deutsches Afrikakorps*, or *Afrika Korps* as it was popularly called. In time, the *Afrika Korps* became a major German component of the *Panzerarmee Afrika* (Panzer Army Africa), which evolved into the German-Italian *Deutsch-Italienische Panzerarmee* and then the *Heeresgruppe Afrika* (Army Group Africa).

Rommel swiftly stabilized the position of the Axis forces in North Africa and drove the British and Commonwealth forces, now re-designated the XIII Corps, back to the borders of Egypt. Rommel's advance was eventually stopped at the First Battle of El Alamein.

A period of comparative inactivity allowed the British to strengthen their forces in Egypt and XIII Corps was incorporated into the new Eighth Army. The 51st (Highland Division) was one of those units sent to reinforce the new army which was led by the enigmatic General Bernard Montgomery.

*

Soon after its arrival in Egypt, the 7th Argylls was posted to a position on the front of the British lines just ahead of El Alamein station. It was here, in a night patrol, that Samwell had his first brush with the enemy. Samwell described his preparations for taking his men out into the night, the pains he took to reconnoitre the ground over which his men would patrol, the feeling of mounting tensions as night approached. To this young Scot, it was a "real adventure". Yet it was the imminent "big attack" that was being planned which he knew would prove the "great test".

That big attack, the Second Battle of El Alamein, began on 23 October 1942. The battalion's CO, Major Lorne MacLaine Campbell (who was awarded the Victoria Cross in 1943 during the fighting in Tunisia), gave this account of the lead-up to Zero Hour:

"Dark came about 7 o'clock on the 23rd and the assembly area then came to life. Everyone emerged from his hole, water bottles were filled, a hot meal was issued from three cook's trucks which had filtered forward at long intervals during the afternoon and final preparations were made. Each man wore a white St Andrew's cross on his back, every other one carried in addition his rifle a pick or a shovel (this for the all-important re-organisation) and everyone had a grenade or two in his pocket.

"At 20.30 hours the march to the start line through prepared gaps in our own two minefields and out on to the tape, laid by the 5th Seaforth in No Man's Land as soon as darkness fell began. All went smoothly and by 21.45 hours, the time at which the infantry had to cross the line, the battalion was formed up ready..

"At 21.40 hours, our artillery opened twenty minutes counter battery work. At 21.45 hours the infantry crossed the start line, peacefully except for the sound of our own guns. At 22.00 hours, Zero Hour, the artillery began their programme on the enemy localities. What happened after that is hard to describe." At least for his men, Samwell provides the reader with a valuable insight.

It was under the cover of this Allied barrage that the men of the 51st (Highland) Division moved forward.

"For the whole time the noise was terrific, and smoke, sand and the smell of cordite everywhere," continued Campbell. "There were minefields to be walked through with care, tripwires attached to anti-personnel mines to the stepped over gingerly (our losses of leaders were probably due partly to them), enemy posts to be attacked and cleared, and over all the colossal din and shells bursting everywhere. The least nice of the number of varied projectiles launched at us was a large affair which burst about thirty feet from the ground with a tremendous flame and shower of sparks. There were also things rather like Chinese Crackers which hopped along the ground banging as they went. But the men were simply marvellous. None of them, even those who had been in France or elsewhere, had ever experienced anything like it before and for most it was their first taste of battle, but they went forward with the Company Pipers playing as steadily as they did in the rehearsals. Casualties were heavy, the heaviest in the Brigade, it not in the Division …"

One of the casualties was Hugh Samwell, one of twelve officers wounded in the battle (another was killed and one listed as missing). "I heard a new sound above the roar of the guns and the explosion of the shells," he recalled. "The sharp rat-tat-tat of Breda and Spandau machine-guns – streams of tracer bullets whined diagonally across our front, not more than twenty yards ahead. We must be getting near to the enemy positions."

With him leading from the front, Samwell's platoon reached the German wire and the enemy's machine-guns opened up just fifteen yards away. "The next second I felt a violent blow on my right thigh. I spun completely round and, recovering my balance, carried on; after going a dozen paces my leg suddenly collapsed under me and I fell forward."

Though wounded, Samwell raised himself up on one arm and urged his men to charge the enemy position. Incredibly, Samwell dragged himself forward, pistol in hand. When he was level with the machine-gun post three Germans jumped up and ran away.

With the British offensive continuing, all that his comrades could do for him was dig a trench and leave him there in the desert – and with him was a wounded Austrian soldier. The two men remained stranded in the desert whilst the German mortars and bullets fell around them all day until, that evening, they were finally found and taken to a field hospital.

Samwell was one of those singled out by his battalion commander as worthy of praise for his actions during the fighting:

"In the turmoil where all did well it was difficult to single out names, but some came in for special notice. Major J.S. Lindsay MacDougall, who with a megaphone in one hand and a rifle slung over his shoulder calmly led his Coy through the hottest fire, and gave a magnificent example of cool and courageous leadership; Lieut. A.M. MacVicar, who, though twice hit, refused to fall out and carried on through the attack and for two days more; Lieut R. Mathieson, who, hit early in the foot, continued to hobble on though he could hardly walk, until another shell smashed his hand and forced him out of the fight, Lieut. H.D.L. Samwell of 'D' Coy, who after the Coy Comdr was hit took charge and was seen everywhere, leading and encouraging his men; L/C Lake of 'C' Coy who turned out a tower of strength, ready to lead anyone and to carry out any order, and a whole host of others."

\*

This exciting, and emotional, start to Samwell's memoir continues with his return to Cairo and a period at an officers' "hardening course" before returning to his battalion at Sirte in January 1943, being posted to 'A' Company. The next night the Highlanders were on the move westwards. General Montgomery had issued his famous declaration "Tripoli in ten days" – the big push was on.

"All that day we tore across the desert, trucks heated up and radiators boiled over," remarked Samwell as he described the Eighth Army's advance across Libya. "Occasionally a truck got stuck in soft sand, another would stop and pull it out, and both would race forward again over the rough desert until they had regained their positions in the column. Sometimes a truck broke down altogether, and the occupants piled into another truck already loaded to capacity."

They pushed on through day and night and, as Montgomery had promised the Eighth Army was in Tripoli within ten days. On 23 January 1943, the Italians surrendered the last city they had occupied during their thirty-year rule of North Africa to what the papers of the day called "The fastest army in history".

This is Samwell's own remarkable account of his part in that victory, a description that ends with his views of the problems of occupation after the Allied landings in Sicily.

Martin Mace and John Grehan
Storrington, 2012

# PREFACE.

My apology, if such is needed, for adding to the many books which have already appeared on the subject of the Eighth Army's victorious advance across Africa and through Sicily to Italy is, that I have not yet seen one which records the experiences and life of the ordinary infantryman—the man who actually meets the enemy in personal combat. This account is based entirely on personal experiences, and I have made no attempt to describe or record actions in which I did not actually take part while out of action wounded.

Neither have I made any attempt to describe the various actions from a tactical point of view, and as I do not wish this account to be mistaken for a history, I have purposely omitted to mention the names of the battalion and division in which I served, though this will be obvious to many who read it. I have criticised where I consider criticism was due, but I wish the reader to understand that criticism of such organisations as A.M.G.O.T. is confined to the areas in which I personally saw the defects—there was much hard and successful work done by this organisation and its forerunner O.E.T.A.

In the chapters which do not deal with battles I have made an attempt to give an accurate and factual account of the conversations which I had with people of various nationalities, but I make no claim that the views expressed necessarily represent those of the person's nation. Through these conversations I have tried to give the reader a true picture of the diverse influences which go to make up that vague term " World Opinion." The characters I have included—Australian, New Zealander, South African, Egyptian, Turk, Jew, Greek, Free French, Giraudist, Petainist, Italian, Palestinian, Indian, Sicilian, German, and American—are all true people, and if perchance I have misquoted them in any detail—though I have taken every care not to, even to the extent of leaving out interesting statements for which I cannot absolutely vouch—I ask them to accept my apologies, for, as they will know, I took no notes, nor did I have any intention of writing a book at the time of meeting them.

# CONTENTS

|       | LEADING FROM THE FRONT | V |
|-------|------------------------|---|
|       | PREFACE | 5 |
|       | FOREWORD | 9 |
| I     | I EMBARK | 11 |
| II    | FIRST IMPRESSIONS OF EGYPT AND ITS WAR-TIME POPULATION | 15 |
| III   | I JOIN THE EIGHTH ARMY | 22 |
| IV    | THE BATTLE OF EL ALAMEIN | 28 |
| V     | THE ATTACK IS RENEWED | 38 |
| VI    | IN A SOUTH AFRICAN HOSPITAL | 51 |
| VII   | IN CAIRO | 55 |
| VIII  | AT THE INFANTRY TRAINING DEPOT AND UP THE LINE | 77 |
| IX    | FROM SIRTE TO TRIPOLI | 93 |
| X     | RESTING IN TRIPOLI | 110 |
| XI    | EARLY DAYS IN FRONT OF THE MARETH LINE | 116 |
| XII   | ROMMEL ATTACKS | 121 |
| XIII  | PATROLS AND KEEPS | 127 |
| XIV   | HOSPITAL IN TRIPOLI | 135 |
| XV    | UP THE LINE AGAIN | 142 |
| XVI   | LEFT OUT OF BATTLE | 146 |
| XVII  | RESTING IN SFAX | 152 |
| XVIII | ENFIDAVILLE AND THE END OF THE CAMPAIGN | 156 |
| XIX   | JOURNEY THROUGH ALGERIA | 162 |
| XX    | TRAINING FOR SEA INVASION | 169 |
| XXI   | FOLLOWING THE SICILY CAMPAIGN FROM AN AFRICAN BASE | 180 |
| XXII  | LANDING IN SICILY AND MOVE TO MESSINA | 184 |
| XXIII | PROBLEMS OF OCCUPATION | 191 |
| XXIV  | THE LIGHTER SIDE OF LIFE ON DETACHMENT | 198 |
| XXV   | LEAVE IN PALERMO | 202 |
|       | EPILOGUE | 209 |
|       | INDEX | 211 |

*In memory of*
Major Hugh Peter de Lancy Samwell MC
8 July 1911 – 12 January 1945

# FOREWORD.

The author of this book is one of those young men of ours—so many of them—who gave their lives to win this victory and this peace. They were precious lives, for among them were thousands with fine intelligence and quality, whose knowledge of life and thoughtfulness had gone deep to the roots of experience because of the things they had seen and done in the neighbourhood of death. War did not brutalise them but ennobled them, because they looked beyond it with a higher vision of human comradeship and civilised ideals, free—if they could help to make it free—from hatred and intolerance and cruelty and beastliness. Such a one was Major Samwell, who has written this narrative of his personal adventures as an infantry officer with the Eighth Army.

I did not know him well, except that sometimes one may know a man well after one talk with him if he opens his heart and mind. When he was in Scotland after being wounded in North Africa he wrote me a long letter, which I read at the breakfast table. It was a remarkable letter, revealing a mind somewhat baffled and hurt by the civilian life around him, to which he had returned for a time. It showed, he thought, a great gap between the spirit of the fighting men and those at home. The wireless news and the war correspondents' despatches had not bridged that gap, he thought, and he was surprised to find a curious indifference and lack of sympathy towards men who had come back expecting more than they received in helpfulness and understanding. I was distressed by this letter but deeply interested in it. It was written by a man of education and thoughtfulness. It was unusual in its psychological analysis. It was rather tragic. I wrote asking him to come and see me if ever he came to London, and not long afterwards we met and talked for a long time. In looks he was a typical young officer of a Scottish battalion. I had met his like a thousand times in the first World War—fresh-complexioned, fair-haired, keen, alert, and, I was glad to find, humorous, though underneath his humour was a serious and sensitive mind. He talked as well as he wrote, and I listened with fascination to his stories about the North African campaign, and especially to that one told in this book, where he lay wounded in a trench with a German soldier more gravely wounded, with whom he talked, without hatred on either side, with death very near to them both. It is, I think, one of the memorable stories of the war.

Major Samwell, as this book shows, was keenly interested in all the characters of life with whom he came in touch. There were no frontiers in his own mind, no narrow national prejudice. He looked out upon life with sympathy for many types and with a keen observation. I told him that he ought to write a book about his experiences, and later he sent me the typescript of this narrative, which I read with much interest and pleasure in its vivid story and varied characters. He told me that he wanted to get back to the front. Much as he hated war he knew that we must win this one for the sake of the world's liberty and civilised ideals, and he pulled every wire he could to get out again when his wound had healed. He went out to France and fought in the great battles which led to victory. He was killed in action on 12th January 1945 in the Ardennes salient, when he was with his old unit, the Argyll and Sutherland Highlanders.

His was one of the lives we can ill spare, and one of the minds who would have helped much in this post-war world by practical idealism and fine feeling. That is the great tragedy of their loss. But by their sacrifice and by their spirit the world has been made free. This book is Major Samwell's own memorial, and he is alive in it.

PHILIP GIBBS.

# CHAPTER I.

### I EMBARK.

It was on the 14th June 1942 that we left Aldershot on the first stage of our journey which was to take us many thousands of miles before we finally returned home in November 1943.

For many weeks before that we had been mobilising and had progressed methodically through the ritual as laid down for troops proceeding overseas. Weeding out of unfits and misfits, inoculations, issue of tropical kit, Inspection by the King, and the final call for certificates that all accounts had been cleared. There was much speculation, of course, as to where we were bound for—the old hands assured us that it was made obvious to them by the type of tropical kit issued, but as no two of these veterans agreed which kit was issued for the Far East or Middle East, we greenhorns were not inclined to take these predictions seriously. The efficiency and organisation by which large bodies of troops are transported from one end of Britain to the other without any noticeable disturbance of normal railway services is amazing.

We entrained at Aldershot one evening and arrived at the Clyde the next afternoon. At various stops on the way hot meals were ready awaiting us, and at no stage of the journey was there any sign of " flapping."

Security, of course, was instilled in all ranks at high pressure for weeks before. I remember how we had all been issued with new divisional and regimental flashes which had been laboriously sewn on for the King's Inspection, only to be taken off again for the journey north. It struck many of us at the time how inconsistent it was to insist with such severity on this matter, and then, for several days while we lay off the Clyde, to permit the troops to lean over the side in full view of the docks with

Balmorals and cap badges proclaiming to all who were interested the regiments and division to which we belonged. We finally sailed in a most imposing convoy, guarded by lively destroyers which raced around us and shot off at angles from time to time. A larger battleship, which we could not see clearly, was also following us.

Our first task on sailing was to sew our flashes on again. They were to come off again and to be re-sewn on twice more before our journey ended!

We had been warned that our living conditions on board were going to be uncomfortable, and, rather unwisely as it turned out, the men had been told that the officers would be the worst off, but I don't think any of us were quite prepared for such crowded conditions.

Unfortunately, after what had been said, the officers, though crowded four in a two-man cabin, were comfortable compared with the men, who were herded like sheep in the depths of the ship, where every conceivable corner had a hammock slung, and yet in spite of this many of the men had to sleep on the tables from which they ate, and even on the floor. When we were to reach the tropics the men were to suffer almost unbearable conditions, but though there was naturally a good deal of grumbling, on the whole they were amazingly good-humoured about it. As they were guided to their quarters some humorist started to imitate a sheep, and this quickly spread until hundreds of men were bleating as they were more or less pushed from one dingy " mess-deck " to another. The first hitch in the otherwise near perfect organisation occurred over this, and for the first two days the whole body of the ship seemed to be a seething mass of cursing humanity pushing and struggling from one side to the other, the congestion and confusion being further aggravated by the necessity of moving bulky kit every time the troops quarter plan was altered. However, we finally settled down, and harassed junior officers got time to inspect their own quarters and pack their kit in every available corner of an overcrowded cabin.

Black-out discipline aboard was very strict, and the

O.C. ship had no hesitation in confining to his quarters, for varying periods, any officer who inadvertently was found smoking on the upper decks after dusk.

The days were spent in boat drill, weapon instruction, and organised games. Officers' instructional classes were run every afternoon. Three weeks passed from the time we left the Clyde until we called in at Freetown. During that time we had almost sailed to within sight of America and back.

There were occasional submarine scares, but on the whole the journey was quite uneventful.

We called in at Cape Town early in July, where we were given a tremendous welcome. Almost every soldier was adopted the moment he set foot on land by a local family who couldn't do too much for him. A big dance was organised for the officers—free cinema and concert shows for the men. On the second day after we docked we went a short route-march, and the townsfolk turned out in hundreds, throwing sweets and chocolate at us and thrusting bags of oranges into our hands. We returned to the ship carrying what seemed to be half the produce of South Africa. Many of the men were adopted as foster-sons at this time, and the good folk afterwards wrote to them and sent parcels throughout the whole campaign. It was winter in Cape Town, the equivalent of a Scottish summer, and the cool air was a welcome change after the almost unendurable heat of the tropical belt.

The short break at Cape Town was over all too soon, and on the fourth day after docking we were on our way again. We still had little or no idea where we were bound for.

We got very little news on board, and what news we did get was almost universally bad. It is interesting to record in view of the " Tell them everything, good or bad " policy afterwards adopted so rigorously by Monty, how fearful the powers were to pass on the news of the fall of Tobruk to the men. I was detailed at that time to give topical talks, and in one of these, in the course of telling the men that Tobruk had fallen, I referred to it as a serious military set-back. This was at once contradicted by a senior officer present, who put over the rather lame excuse that it was all part of our policy to conserve the Mediterranean Fleet. The men, of course, were incredulous, and this effort to sugar the news did nothing but harm. I was, of course, reprimanded, but two days later, when extracts from Churchill's speech were posted on the news board, his words on this subject coincided almost exactly with mine, and the senior officer concerned took the very first opportunity to admit to all that he had been wrong.

We had been eight weeks at sea when we at last entered the Red Sea. It was grilling weather, and the men below decks lay gasping, stripped to the waist, in their crowded quarters. We were to experience worse conditions before we landed. With the enemy almost at the gates of Alexandria it was too risky to allow more than one ship at a time from the convoy to sail through the Suez Canal, and as we appeared to be unlucky in the draw, we were the last, and for a whole week we cruised at very reduced speed round and round a barren island in the Red Sea. While we had been steaming at a steady fourteen knots the breeze had made the heat just bearable, but now there was not the semblance of a breeze to relieve the oppressive glare of the August sun. Day and night we lay and gasped, and it says a lot for the physical fitness of the men and the care of the M.O.s that we had so little illness.

Finally on the 15th August we landed at Port Tewfik, and we then knew we were destined for the Desert.

## CHAPTER II.

### FIRST IMPRESSIONS OF EGYPT AND ITS WAR-TIME POPULATION.

My first impressions of Egypt were by no means favourable. Glaring heat, appalling smells, filthy Arab labourers unloading the ship, and hundreds upon hundreds of screaming children shouting for baksheesh at every station we stopped at on our way to the base camp. We had all been expecting mail to be awaiting us, but there was none, and I think this disappointment added to our depression.

The last part of our journey was by truck, and my truck happened to stop, during a temporary halt, opposite a P.O.W. cage. The German prisoners, wearing the uniform of the Afrika Korps, crowded to the wires and shouted insults at us. One typical Nazi type shouted in good English, " You are just in time to witness Rommel's victory march through Cairo." Another jeered, " More prisoners for the Afrika Korps; why not pack in at once, you haven't a chance, we shall be free within a week." This irritated and to a certain degree depressed us further, for the last news we had heard was far from cheerful.

We arrived at our camp, and the preparations for our reception did nothing to cheer us up.

The first few days were spent in reorganisation and in getting acclimatised to the excessive heat and glaring sand. How we hated those short marches across the interminable sand. We were horribly out of condition after being cooped up for so long, and, unaccustomed as we were to marching on the soft sand, every step was misery.

After about a week we were suddenly moved up to the Nile Delta area. We learnt that Rommel's drive on Cairo and Alexandria was imminent, and that we were to defend the line of the Nile to the last man.

It was a strange feeling—one of expectancy and fear, not so much of the actual battle, but how we as individuals would behave under fire for the first time. It was a relief, however, to see green fields and trees again, and the various journeys we made from one sector to another were packed with interesting and novel experiences.

We had great difficulty in preventing the men, during halts on the march, from accepting fruit and water from the pitchers of the natives. I remember one day, after warning the men repeatedly against drinking this water, I was given a providential opportunity to let them see the reasons for themselves. We were resting during a halt, and I had just caught one of my men drinking deeply from a large pitcher offered to him by a particularly verminous female. On the banks of the Canal, which some humorist had named the Sweet Water Canal—this was its authentic name—an Arab was standing up to the waist in the filthy water going through the actions of washing; a little farther up another Arab was crouched over the edge of the canal, in full view, quite unself-consciously using it as a lavatory. Just at that moment a horribly bloated corpse of a dead donkey floated by in the sluggish current; the exposed belly was floating above water-level and on it thousands of flies were buzzing and settling. Not more than ten yards down the stream from this little scene, four or five women were busy filling their pitchers while others were doing the household laundry. I called the whole company over and let them study the scene while I carefully pointed out each actor in the little drama. I had no further trouble after that in persuading the men not to drink water offered to them by the natives!

During this time we worked feverishly digging trenches for platoon and company positions. The chances of Rommel's men infiltrating through from the south were taken seriously, and we sent out frequent patrols during the night. There was some air activity, and a village half a mile away was bombed by the enemy.

During this time too—it was the last few days of

August—I had two days in Cairo. It was strange and rather exciting to find myself once more in a city, and I made the most of it to purchase various articles which experience had already taught us were necessary for our present life, but it was not the town so much as the people that interested me most. From a seat of vantage in an open-air café I gazed upon the continual flow of people of every type and nationality, and I determined to try and get into conversation with some of them in order to discover their opinions on the present situation. Outwardly Cairo was calm, and life went on normally; but under this surface of indifference one could sense the tension. Looking round me I saw at the next table a group of dapper little French officers of the Free French forces conspicuously wearing the cross of Lorraine. A little farther away was a large table at which a group of men in European civilian clothes were sitting smoking and drinking coffee. They were a very mixed crowd, obviously local business men. It was difficult to place their nationality, but I hazarded a guess that they included Greeks, Jews, a well-to-do Egyptian, and a Turk.

At that moment a party of young English officers, rather foppishly dressed in corduroy trousers, khaki jerseys with leather pocket flaps, open shirts with silk scarves of the blue-and-white spots variety knotted loosely around their necks, entered the restaurant. Most of them sported suede desert boots and had long hair brushed back over their ears. They spoke in loud affected tones and gazed round rather superciliously to find an empty table. A table of Australians on my right started making audible remarks about them of a very derogatory character. I listened with interest and could not help finding myself agreeing with them, and at the same time feeling rather ashamed of my fellow countrymen. They compared very unfavourably with the strong desert-tanned Australians.

We had met a few of these Australians during the past two weeks, and they had been very friendly towards us, and most of them had claimed some Scottish ancestor when welcoming us to the Middle East, but they hadn't troubled to hide from us that they considered us very green, and they looked rather doubtfully at some of our short bandy-legged Glasgow lads. One could read their thoughts easily—" Not tough enough for this kind of war." They smiled at our sun topees and openly derided our military transport march discipline. We were rather proud of this M.T. discipline ; for we had done a lot of training in M.T. moves back home, and took it very seriously. The Australians seemed to tumble anyhow into the first truck they saw ; they smoked in the trucks and lay half undressed sprawled across their kit. They called their officers by their first name and treated even Generals with easy familiarity, but they seemed to get there just the same, and they had fewer hold-ups than we. It made us inclined to reconsider our discipline, and certainly we felt very self-conscious. Later we were to bless our commanders for insisting on it during the advance on Tripoli, but at this time in our efforts to look less green we did everything to avoid it whenever we had the chance.

Meanwhile the young English officers had found a table at the far end of the restaurant, but their voices carried over all the excited chatter and the clattering of plates. Rather shyly I moved over to the next table where the Australians were sitting. There were a captain, two subalterns, and three non-commissioned officers. They replied to my greeting in an offhand manner and carried on with their conversation. They were discussing the recent fighting and arguing over the competence of the Generals and G.H.Q. Opinion seemed to be equally divided ; some blamed the Generals for everything and said very rude things about G.H.Q. ; others said that it wasn't the Generals' fault, it was entirely a question of inferior equipment and arms and too few fighting men. This remark brought them back to the " English twerps." They all agreed that there were far too many of them hanging round G.H.Q., and a little hardship in the desert would do them a world of good if they could stand it, which they doubted very much. I ventured to ask a tall fair-haired sergeant what they thought of the actual English fighting men. They all stopped talking and for the first time took notice of me. I found their appraising stares rather disconcerting. At last one of the subalterns asked not exactly rudely but certainly aggressively, " Are you a blasted newspaper man ? " I hastily assured him I wasn't and told him what division I was in, adding rather unnecessarily that we were newly out. The atmosphere warmed up at once and the sergeant said, " We have heard of you fellows ; God knows we need some real fighters, but I'm afraid you've come too late and you will not have time to get the hang of it." I again asked about the English fighting troops ; there was a silence for a minute and then a corporal said slowly and somewhat grudgingly, " They're not bad what there are of them, but too damn stuck-up." Another said, " You've got to give it to the tank boys though, they are real good, and God what a hell of a time they've had ! " They went on to talk about the South Africans, and some were rather bitter about Tobruk, and hinted that there had been treachery, but all agreed that the majority were good fighters and had made up for it since. Everyone spoke highly of General Neil Ritchie, and they were a bit sore about his being superseded. Monty meant nothing to them ; they had heard that he and Churchill had had a clean-up at G.H.Q. They asked me about Monty. At that time I knew very little about him, but said he was a hell of a man for cross-country runs and general keeping-fit campaigns while at home. They grunted at this, but I couldn't be sure whether it was a grunt of approval or disapproval. They then got up to go and wished me the best of luck ; they were going to " beat up Bardias " (a night club) before returning to the front on the morrow.

Feeling that I was being watched and a little frightened of being taken for a spy, I strolled over to the bar and said " Good morning " to a French officer standing by. He responded at once and, looking at my untanned face, remarked in French, " You are new out, n'est-ce pas ? "

I said I was, and he then offered me a drink. An English staff officer standing by looked disapproving, and I could almost hear him saying, " Gad, the fellow talks to foreigners." I followed the French officer to a table where there were three others sitting. Two were French and one was Greek. I asked them what they thought of the situation; again I got a suspicious glance and they asked if I was a newspaper man. They looked reassured when I told them I was an ordinary infantry officer and was anxious to know what the real situation was. The Greek officer, whose French I could understand better than the Frenchman's, answered. He said things showed signs of improving, but it was a question whether we could stop Rommel if he were really strong enough to attack, but they didn't think he was; they thought he had paid a heavy price for his advance and was short of oil and petrol in particular. This rather surprised me; for I had heard over and over again that Rommel had captured huge stores of our petrol. The Greek went on to say that our Navy and Air Force were accounting for at least half of Rommel's replacements, and he thought Rommel couldn't afford to wait and would attack with what he had and we would be able to hold him. Three days later Rommel did attack, and after a critical time, when part of his armour broke through, and there was nothing between it and the Nile, he was held, and then driven back, losing heavily in tanks. The others agreed with the Greek, but thought we might have to evacuate Alexandria. In contrast to the Australians these men had nothing but praise for our High Command, but perhaps this was in deference to my nationality. They got up to go soon after, and I strolled up to the bar again.

The English staff officer was still there, and he turned to me and offered me a drink and then indicated that we should move over to the corner of the bar. I was surprised; for I thought he had shown clearly his disapproval of my talking to the Frenchman, and from his dress I had mentally put him in the same category as the fops who had so disgusted the Australians. I was quite wrong ; he spoke quietly and without affectation. After a few moments of casual conversation he remarked, " I saw you talking to those Frenchmen ; please don't think I am interfering, but one can't be too careful here. The whole place is hotching with spies. Did they pump you at all ? " I felt, and I'm afraid looked rather guilty, though I had nothing to be guilty about. I gave him the gist of our conversation and he nodded with obvious relief. " You are all right as long as you let them do the talking. I hope you didn't mind my mentioning it." And with a pleasant smile and farewell he left me.

I didn't attempt to approach anyone else, and for the rest of the day I strolled round the streets pestered by shoe-shine boys and beggars. I visited the famous bazaar and didn't think much of it. The Egyptians and local population were not friendly, and showed in an indefinable way that they thought we were finished, and they weren't sorry. It wasn't that anyone said as much, but one felt it all round. The attitude of the shopkeepers and even the shoe-shine boys was rude, offhand, and almost gloating. In one small shop I was surprised to see the Italian flag prominently displayed, with a picture of Mussolini and King Victor Emmanuel on either side. I returned to the unit that evening, and something kept me from repeating my conversations of the morning, even to my friend who shared my views in most things. The next day the " flap " started, and we were all standing-to for the next three days.

## CHAPTER III.

### I JOIN THE EIGHTH ARMY.

SHORTLY after the failure of Rommel's attack we moved forward to an area behind the front on ground that had already been fought over in the recent battle. Here we practised day and night for what we now know was the Battle of El Alamein. It was a gruelling and testing time; we were suffering from all the usual diseases that afflict new troops when they first arrive in the Middle East—dysentery, " gyppy tummy," sand-fly fever, desert jaundice.

We lived in boxes—*i.e.*, large areas capable of holding a complete brigade, boxed in on all sides by minefields, with two or three recognised exits. We were beginning to get used to the sun, but the flies were appalling; one couldn't raise a piece of bread and jam from plate to mouth without it becoming covered in flies. They buzzed round one's head, eyes, mouth, and ears. Every precaution was taken with food, latrines, &c., but it was difficult to stop men from throwing rubbish away or even not using the latrines during the night, when they had to go anything up to fifteen times, and at night it was quite possible to get lost by moving even fifty yards from one's " bivy," so completely featureless was the desert. One often felt convinced one was making direct for one's " bivy," only to find oneself completely lost in another company area. Those of us who had compasses used to take a bearing on the latrines. This was a wretched time; the training was dreadfully hard and monotonous, and nearly all of us were feeling ill to varying degrees.

Some officers went up to the front during this time; they were attached to the Australians. Things were very quiet up there, and they came back with amazing stories of men strolling about in full view of the enemy, but they emphasised that the war was taken seriously at night and there was constant patrolling. As in other things military, the Australians were very unorthodox in their patrolling methods. They hardly bothered about compasses but went from point to point by means of battle landmarks, utilising everything from broken-down tanks to unburied corpses. One company had a skeleton whom they affectionately called "Cuthbert," who was propped up with his arm pointing to the gap in our minefield. Coming back from patrols it was one of the most difficult things to find these gaps, and, as most patrols were timed to end just before dawn, one couldn't afford to waste time walking up and down trying to find the gap and thus risk being caught in the open during stand-to, thus inviting a burst of machine-gun fire.

Early in October we took over a sector of the front just beyond Alamein Station—a single railway line passed through the forlorn "station," which consisted of a broken signal and a hut and wooden platform wrecked by a shell. After the station the road which ran parallel deteriorated into little more than a track. On the north of the line there was a further expanse of rough desert interspersed with a kind of gorse, then the main road to Mersah-Matruh, a thoroughly modern tarred highway. On the far side of this there were cliffs leading down to the long stretch of white sand which bordered the sea.

Life at the front at this time was very quiet and rather unreal. We welcomed the rest from the gruelling training, and wished we could remain there indefinitely. Everything went according to a programme which was kept by both sides. Stand-to followed by another short sleep, then just before breakfast the enemy would put over a few shells which landed somewhere in the back area, occasionally frightening Battalion H.Q. but otherwise doing little harm. This was replied to by our own artillery, and then there was complete silence; gradually men emerged from the trenches and started brewing up and visiting each other. The enemy did the same; their advance posts were some three thousand yards away, but as the ground was completely flat, on a clear day one could quite easily see them. Neither side took the least notice of the other and went about their morning tasks. Water had to be brought up in cans from the water-point at El Alamein Station; men and positions had to be inspected; and all the other routine jobs of an infantry company. We even did a little weapon training. By mid-day it was very hot and we had our siesta and light tiffin, then we went off in parties for a bathe. The trenches, old ones and very solid, had once been a Corps H.Q. when the front was on the Egyptian border; they were flea-ridden and even lice were evident. Jerry over the other side also went out for a swim, and sometimes we could spot them jumping about in the water. We had our big meal in the evening and then spent the rest of the time preparing for patrols.

Patrols at that time were a real adventure, and brigade staff, and particularly the Brigade Intelligence Officer, were even more excited about them than we were, but they hadn't to go out! I remember the first patrol I took out—the feeling of tension for hours before, the pains I took to reconnoitre from forward positions and prepare the men, even to the laying on of a hot cup of tea on our return. All according to the book! The I.O. gave me a most elaborate story—proceed 1000 paces W. bearing 180, then 400 paces S.W. bearing 110, &c., &c., —and all this for the general purpose of finding out what activity, if any, there was on that particular sector of the enemy's front. It was a recce patrol, and we had strict orders to avoid a fight if possible and on no account to give away who we were. I was ordered to take twenty men with me, and even at that early stage I realised how foolish and unnecessary it was to take so many men on that type of patrol. Three of us would have been quite sufficient, and we could have done the job far more quietly and efficiently. Afterwards, until I was allowed to choose my own men and numbers, I used to leave the greater part of the patrol detailed just outside our minefield and do the job in half the time with an N.C.O. and batman. We set off about 9 P.M.; the weather had broken and there was a gale blowing and heavy rain. We were in K.D. with no coats. Although the patrol was not to start till midnight, we had been ordered to report at the advance positions by 10 P.M., and so for two hours we lay in slit trenches getting soaked to the skin and shivering with cold. I spent the time reconnoitring the mine-gap and memorising any landmarks. I was later to thank my lucky stars I did. We started off dead on midnight; the wind had dropped a bit and the rain had ceased, but by this time we were soaked through. We clattered over the rocky ground, making, it seemed to me, enough noise to awaken the dead. After about an hour, during which we found a tank full of corpses and a blown-up German truck with the dead driver still at the wheel, and had lain doggo while what we thought was an enemy patrol passed through their own minefield gap, we found ourselves at the enemy wire. We could hear them talking quite clearly, and the sound of trucks moving up and being unloaded.

We lay for a bit listening, and then I decided to go forward with three men. I knew I was committing a military crime by splitting my patrol, but it would have been madness to take twenty unskilled men with me right through the enemy forward positions. I still shudder when I think how innocently I took such a grave risk. I had vaguely heard of anti-personnel mines, but somehow it never struck me that by climbing over the wire I was walking right into a minefield plentifully sprinkled with anti-tank and anti-personnel mines. Beginners' luck was with me, however, and I got right through without incident. I lay beside a truck of sorts and listened to two German sentries talking. I caught snatches of their conversation. One was complaining of the cold, and the other remarked that he would have had something really to grumble at if he had been on the Russian front as the speaker had been last year. In the distance men were singing while unloading petrol and water-cans. It was the first of many times that I was to hear that haunting little melody introduced by the Germans and later adopted by us, " Lili Marlene."

Having plotted my position and feeling I had carried out all my instructions, I started crawling back, closely followed by the two men. Again luck was with us and we got through the minefield safely, but unfortunately I tripped over the wire and there was a terrible clatter. A challenge rang out, followed by excited voices calling, and then two shots were fired in my direction. I heard the bullets singing over my head, and we didn't wait for more. Collecting the rest of the patrol we made off as quickly as possible, sacrificing silence for speed. Oddly enough no more shots were fired, and we reached our own wire without further incident, but our troubles weren't over—I couldn't find the gap. Up and down I ran trying to recognise some familiar object. Time passed and it was getting light, the men were growing anxious, and to make matters worse the rain had started again. Almost in a panic I stopped to cool off and think, and then I saw the high triple dannert on my right tapering off to a single coil, and I remembered that that was the beginning of the gap. With great relief I led the men through, and finally got back to our own lines. The men's work was now finished and they immediately turned in, but I had my report to make out, and it had to be in to Brigade by 8 A.M. I wrote frantically by the light of a torch and drew a rough sketch-map; then, not having the heart to wake my snoring batman, I took the report back to Battalion H.Q. myself. I was dead tired; the reaction from the nervous tension had set in, but over it all I had a feeling of real satisfaction and a new confidence in myself.

The report duly reached Brigade, and apparently met with approval, though I was awakened after an hour's sleep to answer the phone. The Brigade I.O. wanted to know how many yards I reckoned 2014 paces were. I'm afraid I was rather short in giving him my reply.

After a few more days we moved out of the line again and put the finishing touches to our training and preparation. We all knew the big attack was imminent. A few days later we moved up to our battle positions—our great test lay ahead.

## CHAPTER IV.

### THE BATTLE OF EL ALAMEIN.

It was part of the battle plan that Rommel should be made to expect that the main attack would come in the south across the ground recently fought over in his own attack. In order to strengthen that belief the whole division and many others were first moved south, where we camped in an area which had been made to look as obviously as possible like a concentration area. Dummy trucks and tanks were scattered about, and large numbers of real trucks and armoured cars were concentrated here. The German reconnoitring planes duly came over and reported these concentrations; then on the night of the 22nd-23rd October we quietly moved back north and took up positions already dug for us just behind the front. Strict orders were given that there was to be no movement after dawn, and for a whole day we had to lie cramped in temporary slit trenches waiting for night. We could not even move out to relieve nature, and one can imagine the discomfort we suffered.

The tension was almost unbearable and the day dragged terribly. I spent the time going over and over again the plan of attack, memorising codes and studying the over-printed map which showed all the enemy positions —the result of weeks of patrolling and reconnaissance from the air. I remember I also read a book which I had just received by mail from home: it was called 'They Died with their Boots on,' a story of the last stand of the Guards in the Battle of France. Not very suitable literature for the occasion. Oddly enough, though keyed up, I did not feel any fear at this time, rather a feeling of being completely impersonal, as if I were waiting as a spectator for a great event in which I was not going to take any active part.

After dark there was tremendous activity: last-minute

visits by commanders and minor adjustments in plans. And then a hot meal was brought up. Most of us were too excited to eat much, but I felt better after I had had some hot soup. I remember the C.O. coming round to wish us all good luck before we went forward to the start line. Knowing how vital it was to keep our water-bottles filled and how uncertain the chances of filling up again were if we drank any during the day, I had filled an empty whisky bottle with water, and was busy drinking it down just as he arrived. He looked at the bottle and jumped to the natural conclusion. He didn't say anything, but showed his disapproval and then was gone before I could explain. This worried me so much that the ordeal ahead seemed quite minor in comparison.

About 9 P.M. we moved forward and took up our positions on the start line—a taped line stretching across the open desert just in front of the forward positions. It was deathly still and a full moon lighted the bleak sand as if it were day. Suddenly the silence was broken by the crash of a single gun, and the next moment a mighty roar rent the air and the ground shook under us as salvo after salvo crashed out from hundreds of guns. Shells whined over our heads in a continuous stream, and soon we saw the enemy line lit up by bright flashes. One or two fires broke out and the ground became clearer than ever. It seemed a long time before the enemy started to reply, but finally they did so, weakly at first, then gradually growing in strength. I could imagine the German gunners having just settled in for another quiet night's sleep, tumbling out of their bivies bewildered and still half asleep. Some of them would never reach their guns, and others would arrive to find their guns blown sky high.

Still I felt the same impersonal air of a spectator, rather as if I were watching the Aldershot Tattoo, and I almost expected to see scarlet-uniformed troops appearing on the horizon depicting the scenes of a long-past battle. Both sides were concentrating on each other's gun-sites, and no shells landed anywhere near us. Time passed and the firing continued, sometimes dying down only to start again with increased intensity; then suddenly I noticed a difference—our shells were now passing very close over our heads and bursting, it seemed to me, only a couple of hundred yards ahead. It was the signal to prepare to advance; our guns were now shelling the enemy's forward positions. I looked at my watch and saw there was still three minutes to go. I felt ice cool, and remember feeling very grateful that I was. Oddly enough I don't remember the actual start—one moment I was lying on my stomach on the open rocky desert, the next I was walking steadily as if out for an evening stroll, on the right of a long line of men in extended order. To the right I could dimly see the tall thin figure of the major commanding the other forward company. He had a megaphone, and was shouting down the line, " Keep up there on the left—straighten up the line." I turned to my batman, who was walking beside me, and told him to run along the line and tell the sergeant in charge of the left-hand platoon to keep his direction from the right.

I suddenly discovered that I was still carrying my ash stick. I had meant to leave it at the rear Company H.Q. with the C.Q.M.S. and exchange it for a rifle. I smiled to myself to think I was walking straight towards the enemy armed only with a .38 pistol and nine rounds of ammunition. Well, it was too late to do anything about it now, but I expected that someone would soon be hit and I could take his. I began to wonder, still quite impersonally, who it would be; perhaps myself! in which case I wouldn't need a rifle. Then I heard a new sound above the roar of the guns and the explosion of shells. The sharp rat-tat-tat of Breda and Spandau machine-guns—streams of tracer bullets whined diagonally across our front, not more than twenty yards ahead. We must be getting near the first enemy positions. I asked the pace-checker on my right how many paces we had done. He grinned and said he had lost count; then crump-crump-crump! a new sharper note. This was something that affected us—mortar shells were landing right among us. I heard a man on my left say, "Oh, God!" and I saw him stagger and fall. The major was shouting again. I couldn't hear what he said, but his company seemed to be already at grips with the enemy. At that moment I saw a single strand of wire ahead about breast high. I took a running jump at it and just cleared it. My sergeant, coming behind, started to climb over it, and immediately there was a blinding flash and a blast of air struck me on the back of the neck. I never saw that sergeant again. I remember wondering what instinct had made me jump that wire. Strange? I hadn't been thinking of booby-traps. We had broken into a run now—why, I don't know. Nobody had given any order. A corporal on my left was firing his Bren gun from the hip. I wondered if he was really firing at anything. Then suddenly I saw a head and shoulders protruding from a hole in the ground. I had already passed it and had to turn half round. I fired my pistol three times, and then ran on to catch up the line.

The line had broken up into blobs of men all struggling together; my faithful batman was still trotting along beside me. I wondered if he had been with me while I was shooting. My runner had disappeared, though; and then I saw some men in a trench ahead of me. They were standing up with their hands above their heads screaming something that sounded like "Mardray." I remember thinking how dirty and ill-fitting their uniforms were, and smiled at myself for bothering about that at this time. To my left and behind me some of the N.C.O.s were rounding up prisoners and kicking them into some sort of formation. I waved my pistol at the men in front with their hands up to sign them to join the others. In front of me a terrified Italian was running round and round with his hands above his head screaming at the top of his voice. The men I had signalled started to come out. Suddenly I heard a shout of "Watch out!" and the next moment something hard hit the toe of my boot and bounced off. There was a blinding explosion, and I staggered back holding my arm over my eyes instinctively. Was I wounded ? I looked down rather expecting to see blood pouring out, but there was nothing—a tremendous feeling of relief. I was unhurt. I looked for the sergeant who had been beside me ; he had come up to take the place of the one who had fallen. At first I couldn't see him, and then I saw him lying sprawled out on his back groaning. His leg was just a tangled mess. I realised all at once what had happened : one of the enemy in the trench had thrown a grenade at me as he came out with his hands up. It had bounced off my boot as the sergeant shouted his warning, and had exploded beside him. I suddenly felt furious ; an absolute uncontrollable temper surged up inside me. I swore and cursed at the enemy now crouching in the corner of the trench ; then I fired at them at point-blank range —one, two, three, and then click ! I had forgotten to reload. I flung my pistol away in disgust and grabbed a rifle—the sergeant's, I think—and rushed in. I believe two of the enemy were sprawled on the ground at the bottom of the square trench. I bayoneted two more and then came out again. I was quite cool now, and I started looking for my pistol, and thinking to myself there will be hell to pay with the quartermaster if I can't account for it. At the same time I wondered when I had got rid of my stick, as I couldn't remember dropping it. I felt rather sad ; it had been my constant companion for two years at home. I had walked down to the pictures with my wife and had put it under the seat, and on leaving I had forgotten it, and had had to disturb a whole row of people to retrieve it. I started then to wonder what my wife was doing at that moment.

The firing had died down and groups of men were collecting round me rather vaguely ; just then a man shouted and fired a single round. I afterwards learnt that one of the enemy in the trench had heaved himself up and was just going to fire into my back when my man saw him and shot him first. I didn't realise what had happened at the time.

Our orders were to consolidate for fifteen minutes

before moving on. I suddenly wondered what had happened to Company Headquarters and my company commander. He and I were the only two officers, commander and second-in-command. We had agreed that he should bring up Company H.Q. and the reserve platoon behind, while I led the forward platoons. I started to walk back, and at that moment the strange lull was abruptly ended by four shells exploding all round me. One covered me in sand, but I wasn't hurt; I found the company commander sitting on the ground trying to get through to Battalion H.Q. on the wireless. I gave him a quick report, but he was only half listening and still trying to get through. The commanding officer appeared from nowhere and asked him how things were going; the company commander replied and then turned to me. I told them we had taken the position and the men were lying resting and watching a few yards in front of the position. The commanding officer said "Good work," and disappeared. The company-commander said, "My God, you have left some pretty sights behind you; what was it like? I haven't fired a shot yet." I was quite surprised that he had seen the result of our fight, for I hadn't realised that we had been still advancing while fighting and had thought that the only positions had been those I had just left in front. I asked him to give me the reserve platoon and I would detail the right forward platoon to drop into reserve. I realised that there were very few of them left. He agreed, and I went forward again.

The stretcher-bearers were at work carrying the wounded to the battalion line of advance between the two forward companies. I remember reorganising the forward platoons, but again don't remember actually starting forward; I just found myself on the move. I heard the other company's piper starting to play just before we had bumped the enemy, and I wondered what had happened to our piper. I sent my new runner back to ask for him, but he never arrived, and the runner didn't return either. Afterwards I learnt he was wounded on the way.

All this time shells were landing among us, but suddenly there was a new danger; I realised we were walking into our own barrage; shells were screaming above our heads and landing just in front of us. The platoon commander of the left platoon of the other company came across to me just at that moment and remarked, " We're going too fast; those are our shells, aren't they?" I agreed, and he went over to the major, his company commander, and warned him. At first the latter wouldn't agree to stop, but at that moment more shells of our own guns landed just in front and we felt the blast. I went across and persuaded him that we were ahead of time. We agreed to stop.

I pulled my men back a few yards to get completely out of the danger zone, and sent word back to my company commander asking him to come up closer. There was only supposed to be fifty yards between forward platoons and Company H.Q. and I couldn't see him. The runner reported that he couldn't find either the company commander or Company H.Q. or the reserve platoon. While my attention was on this, the other company had decided to advance again as the barrage had lifted. I didn't see them go and they failed to warn me. I found myself out in the " blue " alone with about forty men. I went over to the left flank to find out what had happened to the regiment that was supposed to be there. They weren't there, and I learnt afterwards that they never got past the first minefield.

My first feelings on realising that the company on my right had carried on without me was one of intense irritation, but when I discovered there was no one on my left either, my anger turned to fear. For the first time that night I was afraid; a nauseating wave of terror went right through me as I realised I was quite alone with the remains of two platoons; my company commander and Company H.Q. had disappeared together with the wireless; the " pilot " officer must have gone with the other company (we were sharing him). Instinct told me that I had gone too far to the left. All this time we had been steadily advancing again, and I started to swing to the right. I was still scared stiff, not at the shells that were exploding round us, but at the thought of being all alone, cut off from the battalion and even my Company H.Q. I was to find—and so was the battalion later—that the failure of the unit on my left to keep up was to cost us dearly. We came to another enemy position; they surrendered without fighting, and we didn't waste time mopping up. I was so anxious to make contact with someone again. It appeared that many of the enemy at this position scuttled down the trenches to the left and remained in the gap where the unit on my left should have been, until we had passed, and then filtered back and shot up the reserve companies and Battalion H.Q. who were coming up behind. I was to be blamed for not finishing them off, but if I had attempted to chase them right across a battalion front I should have been hopelessly lost, while at the same time failing to secure my own objective.

I was still feeling terribly afraid and lonely when I heard a shout behind, and up came a platoon of the reserve company under the second-in-command, and with them was the remains of my own Company H.Q. What a wave of relief swept over me! Immediately the fear vanished. I had someone to discuss the position with. It appeared that a shell landed right among my Company H.Q. just after I had left it, badly wounding the company commander and laying out the signals; however, the reserve company's platoon had a wireless with them, so we were all right. The platoon commander told me I was still too far to the left, and we wheeled half-right. Soon we came to another enemy position, which we recognised as our final objective. The enemy put up a half-hearted fight here, but soon gave in; but most of them escaped to the left again, and again I didn't consider it advisable to chase them with the few men I had left. We advanced a further 300 yards and then started to dig in. There was still no sign of the other company, but I was quite convinced I was in the right place. I got through to Battalion H.Q. by wireless and reported myself in position. The officer who had joined me went off to reconnoitre, and returned shortly to say that the other forward company was already dug in 200 yards on our right. I felt elated by this news. It was almost dawn before we were finally dug in. We were left completely unmolested by the enemy, and our own and their artillery had stopped firing. Apart from the occasional sounds of small-arms fire well to our right, everything was very peaceful. After stand-to I posted sentries, and leaving my company sergeant-major in charge settled into a trench with the two signallers of the reserve company's platoon and went to sleep. The officer commanding the reserve platoon dug in near me.

I was wakened at 8.30 A.M. by my batman with some " breakfast "—half a tin of bully, two biscuits, and a mug of water. I made out reports of casualties, and then, crouching down gingerly, made my way towards the position which had been pointed out to me as Battalion H.Q. Gradually, as there was no sign of firing, I became more daring, and ended by walking normally up to the trench which the commanding officer and adjutant were sharing. It was very small, and their legs were all mixed up together. Just at that moment a tank away on the right started firing, and the shells whistled unpleasantly close by over my head. I hastily jumped into the trench, squatting precariously on the combined legs of the two occupants. I told the commanding officer the main events of the previous night and gave him the casualties, which were high. The adjutant offered me a swig of rum, and after he had pointed out where the ammunition dump was, I started back to the company, passing through the other forward company on the way and stopping a moment to compare notes. There was no sign of the enemy, though I was to learn later that they were less than 300 yards away. When I returned to my own trench, the signallers, against all rules, had switched on to the B.B.C., and we had the strange experience of hearing the folk at home being told that the "Eighth Army had attacked, and the battle was progressing favourably and according to plan." So ended the first phase of the Battle of El Alamein.

## CHAPTER V.

### THE ATTACK IS RENEWED.

ABOUT mid-day on Sunday, 25th October, the commanding officer called a conference; it was obvious to all that our position was precarious so long as the left flank remained exposed. It was decided that one reserve company should stride across the mouth of this gap and capture the original objective of the unit which had still failed to put in an appearance, thus bottling up an enemy element still left in the gap, and at the same time making contact with the unit which had gained its objective on the far side.

The attack was to be made early in the afternoon, but was cancelled at the last moment in favour of a three-company night attack timed for 10 P.M. that night. We returned to our company areas, and at this time the major who had led the company on my right was wounded by shrapnel. The loss of officers was already serious; the two original forward companies had two officers between them—myself and one captain transferred from the right reserve company. This company had a company commander and one subaltern left; the fourth company had been split up. One platoon, the one that had joined me the previous night under the second-in-command, was still with me; the rest of the company which had been detailed to come up on the tanks had disappeared together with the tanks. I learnt later that they had been held up by an unexpectedly large and uncharted minefield. The total strength of the rifle companies available was not more than 150 all ranks. Our senior N.C.O. casualties had been heavy also.

We lay in our holes during the afternoon; there was desultory shelling and mortar fire; some tanks came up, and, moving forward to a rise in the ground ahead of us, lined up as if for a review, and we were further depressed by the sight of one after the other being potted off like the sitting ducks they were. In the late afternoon, while we were dozing in our holes, the enemy mortar fire suddenly grew in intensity and shells exploded all round us. At first I thought it was a prelude to the expected counter-attack, but soon we were amazed to see a company of another battalion advancing in extended line diagonally across our front, parallel to the main enemy positions. As they came level with us the enemy opened up with machine-guns to support their mortars, and bullets hissed angrily over our heads as we crouched in our holes, occasionally peeping gingerly over the top to watch this extraordinary and unexpected performance. I was to learn later that our own H.Q. were as mystified as we were. Two or three men of this advancing force fell close to our positions, and we crawled out to pull them into our holes. When they had advanced about two hundred yards beyond us, they went to earth and burrowed themselves in. We never saw them again, and to this day I do not know how they came to be there.

The rest of the day passed uneventfully and at 9.30 P.M. we prepared to move to the start-line. Some rum had come up, but there was not enough for each man to get the regulation tablespoon swig. Most of the N.C.O.s and myself had to stand down. Just after we arrived at the start-line the two platoons of the missing company came up, and the platoon which had been with me left to rejoin its company. I had now only thirty-two men, a company sergeant-major, two corporals, and myself. I was in the centre with the two original reserve companies on each flank. It was brilliant moonlight and we must have been seen by the enemy before we started; also the last-minute arrival of the last company, and the other reserve company being on the start-line, caused a certain amount of noise and confusion, and before we started the enemy were firing at us.

We started to advance; this time we had no artillery support, for the object had been to surprise the enemy. An officer in a reconnoitring car had reported earlier that the position was only lightly held by frightened Italians who had tried to surrender to him, but as he was alone and under heavy shell-fire, he had been unable to stay to round them up. This was cheering news and we advanced confidently. We had only gone a few yards when streams of machine-gun tracer bullets whistled across our front, intersecting at a point about 100 yards directly ahead of us. The enemy were firing across our front on fixed lines; some mortars added to our discomfort, but we pressed on. It was a strange feeling approaching the first almost continuous stream of machine-gun tracer, knowing that the next step would take us into it; we crossed it with a few casualties, but looking to my flanks I discovered I was again alone, and the fear of the night before returned with the same sickening intensity. We could hear sounds of heavy firing and shouting on our left, and I guessed that the left-hand company had run into some enemy positions. There was no sign at all from the right-hand company.

We continued to advance, and then ahead I saw barbed wire: breaking into a trot we jumped over and started to rush the positions we now saw clearly ahead. We saw German helmets, and I cursed that reconnoitring officer for his misleading information. A machine-gun opened up not more than fifteen yards half left from me; I saw the tracer bullets coming straight for me and I could clearly see the heads and shoulders of the three men manning the gun. The next second I felt a violent blow on my right thigh. I spun completely round and, recovering my balance, carried on; after going a dozen paces my leg suddenly collapsed under me and I fell forward. The men following, mistaking my involuntary action for intention, followed suit, and we lay there, about a dozen of us, not more than twenty yards from the enemy with bullets whistling over our heads. Although I found I couldn't get up, I felt no pain, and raising myself on one arm I shouted for them to rush in at the bayonet point. They did not respond at once; I think they were waiting for me to get up, and there were no N.C.O.s left. Then a corporal from the reserve section doubled up to me and asked what was happening. Almost incoherent with anger at the delay which was making our chances of taking the position less likely every moment, for the enemy were bound to realise soon how few there were of us, I shouted " Get in," and for the first time I remember I swore at my men. The company sergeant-major came up at that moment, and at the same time something little short of a miracle happened. The enemy shouted to us, and we saw that they had their hands up. The men jumped up and rushed in, and I dragged myself after them.

As I drew level with the machine-gun post three Germans jumped out and ran off as hard as they could. I had my pistol in my hand (I must have dropped my rifle when I fell). I fired four times, and saw one pitch forward on his face. The men then returned for me and carried me into a deep dug-out and laid me on a bunk beside other wounded. The blankets were still warm from the bodies of the Germans who had been sleeping there. There was a tin of cold coffee on the floor, and a stretcher-bearer gave me a drink.

The company sergeant-major came in and reported that they had rounded up prisoners, including one officer. I asked him to help me out so that I could supervise the defence and interview the officer prisoner. I knew I must get some information at once, for we were in a dangerous position. At first the German wouldn't talk and I had to use a little persuasion ; it was no time for niceties. Finally I learnt that they were an Austrian unit with German officers and that they had been rushed up to relieve the Italians that evening after dusk ; so the reconnoitring officer's report was true after all.

Just then I saw some of our own men and recognised the company sergeant-major of the right-hand company. He was going off at an angle beyond the position. I shouted to him to come over, but he shouted something I couldn't hear and carried on ; then I heard shouting on my left, and the left-hand company came rushing in. I shouted for an officer, for I wanted to hand over quickly as I was feeling very faint. A subaltern came over and rather indignantly asked me what I wanted, saying I was keeping him back from the fighting. I answered rather irritably that the fighting was all over and I wanted him to take over the defence for the inevitable counter-attack which I was expecting any moment. He still answered aggressively, " Why the hell can't you do it ? I have my own platoon to look after." The German officer was still standing by, and I felt furious that he should hear this stupid squabbling and prayed he couldn't understand English. I answered angrily, " I order you to take over at once. I am wounded." He said, " Oh ! Sorry, I didn't realise." He went off and I lay down again, but I wasn't happy in this dug-out. I felt too closed in and wanted to know what was happening, and if we were to be overrun in the expected counter-attack I wanted a chance to defend myself. I called to my batman, and he helped me out and dug me a shallow hole on the perimeter of a slight rise. He brought me a Bren gun and told me that the company commander of the left company was organising all-round defence and there was no need to worry. I felt much happier with the gun and fired a few rounds to make sure it was O.K. There was a good deal of movement going on on my right, but I couldn't see anything. I heard what I thought was a carrier, and shortly after an N.C.O., who had gone out to reconnoitre on his own initiative, came back to report that there were two enemy anti-tank guns about 300 yards out, and he thought they were preparing to fire on us. I told him to pass on this information to the left-hand company commander who was now in charge : he did so and returned shortly to say with disgust, " He isn't taking any action." I was puzzled, but I knew this company commander was an excellent officer and so presumed there was some reason.

The counter-attack didn't materialise, and later on I got two men to carry me farther into the perimeter, where they prepared a deep trench for me. Shortly after a wounded German was brought in. I got the men to bring him up to my trench and started to question him. He answered very listlessly; told me he was an Austrian, he was too old for active fighting, and that the officers were all Germans and they didn't get on with them. He kept asking when the doctor would be coming. The original plan was for Battalion H.Q. to move forward after us and come up when we had taken the position, so I told him quite cheerfully that we would both be safely in hospital before dawn. This cheered him up a lot, and he said he was glad he was out of it all. He told me he was a machine-gunner and pointed to the post where I had seen the three men running out, and I remembered I had shot one. I asked him where he was wounded, and he said, " In the back." This struck me as a coincidence; perhaps he was the very man that shot me and perhaps I had shot him, and now we were talking together like polite strangers in a railway carriage.

At this moment the enemy, who had obviously heard that we had captured the position, started mortaring us. It was deadly accurate and most uncomfortable. A trench nearby, with some light casualties in it, got a direct hit; it wasn't a pleasant sight. The Austrian dragged himself into the other half of my trench; I didn't stop him. We lay in silence together for a long time, and I think I dozed off; at any rate I suddenly realised he was speaking to me again. " Wann kommt der arzt ? " he almost whined. I answered rather impatiently, " Oh, he'll be here soon." Then he said something I couldn't understand, but he pointed at my drill shorts, and I realised that they were soaked in blood. He stretched across, obviously in considerable pain, and I tried to stop him, but he insisted. Apparently the bullet had gone through the fleshy part of the thigh, coming out at the other side, and when the stretcher-bearer had hastily bandaged me he had placed the field dressing on the place where the bullet had entered, whereas of course it was bleeding from the place of exit. With great difficulty the Austrian bandaged it again, using his own field dressing. I felt rather guilty for having spoken so abruptly to him, and when he had finished I did my best to dress his wound. It was a bullet wound right between the shoulder-blades, and the bullet was still in. It was hardly bleeding at all and there was little I could do. I gave him my haversack as a pillow and he was pathetically grateful. I asked him if he was married, and he immediately started to fumble in his tunic pocket and brought out the inevitable family photo. His " Frau " was a typical Austrian hausfrau type ; there were three children—a girl of about twelve, a boy of perhaps ten, dressed in local costume, and a little girl of three or four. I duly admired them and asked him what he did in civilian life. I thought it was a good thing for both of us to talk about things that would keep our minds off our present situation. He chattered on, occasionally stopping for a deep breath, which appeared to give him considerable pain. I found it very difficult to follow him, because he had a broad Austrian accent and " swished " his " ch's " and ran words into each other. He appeared to be a cotton worker from Linz ; he had been called up about a year ago for home defence work, for he was thirty-seven ; then suddenly a month ago he was drafted out to Benghazi with some very young Austrian boys. He was quite sure a mistake had been made, but nobody would listen to him ; he had been made an orderly and had only arrived at the front with a draft of reinforcements the day before. He had been detailed to a machine-gun crew that afternoon and had only been in position two hours before we arrived. He had never fired a machine-gun before that night.

I thought to myself how interesting this information would be to the Higher Command, and made a mental note to report it as soon as I reached hospital. Hospital ! What a thought ! Clean beds, regular meals, ample water, sleep, peace from this infernal noise. Would I ever get there ? A wave of terror swept over me. Supposing I was killed before they got me out. Oh, God !

don't let that happen. I quickly switched my mind back to the Austrian and almost shouted at him, " Do you ski ? " He said, " Yes," and we talked ski-ing for the next five minutes. I remembered spending a night at Linz on my honeymoon while we were motoring to Vienna. I told him I thought it was a dull depressing place. I talked feverishly, struggling to remember my German. I don't think he understood half I said, but I had to talk to keep my mind off realities ; then I saw he was asleep. I relaxed, and suddenly I felt very tired.

The dawn was just breaking, and I thought to myself, " Well, I am excused stand-to this morning." I must have slept for three hours. I had dreadful dreams. One minute I was at home, and someone was continually hitting me on the thigh, and I was too weak to stop them. My hands appeared to be tied behind my back. Then I was back in the desert. We were on route-march, and I had fallen out to relieve nature. I was trying to run to catch up with the company, which was fast disappearing. My legs were dreadfully weighted and I could scarcely move ; that terror of being alone in the desert came over me. There was a huge scorpion on my thigh, and it was viciously stabbing me with its poisoned tail. I kept trying to push it off, and thought I had, but it was still there. I was desperately thirsty, and my water-bottle was empty. I was then back in our bathroom at home, and my wife was filling the bath with cool clear water. I cried out and cupped my hands to drink, but the water kept running out. I begged her to fetch a cup, but she laughed and said the children were using the only cups ; then I woke up. The sun was glaring down on me in its full intensity. It was very silent. I was perspiring all over. My mouth was horribly dry and had a dreadful taste. I felt for my water-bottle ; I remembered I had unstrapped it to give the Austrian a drink. It was only half full, but I knew I had my reserve bottle in my haversack under the Austrian's head. Then in horror I remembered that I had taken it out the night before while in the dug-out to give a wounded man a drink. Had I put it back ? I couldn't remember. It was a pity to disturb the Austrian when he was sleeping so peacefully; but was he sleeping ? I looked at him again ; his skin was all drawn in and he was deathly white. Had he died in the night ? I stretched over and felt his pulse ; it was beating weakly. He stirred and murmured, " Wann kommt der Arzt ? " I replied, " Bald," and he sighed and went to sleep again. I carefully pulled the haversack from under his head and substituted my army pullover which I had taken off. He stirred, but didn't wake up. I feverishly opened the haversack—my worst fears were realised ! I had left my reserve bottle in the dug-out. I shook my issue bottle ; it was less than half full. I drank very slowly, and then, filling my mouth, washed it out, spitting the water back into my bottle. I didn't feel like eating ; I had a packet of hard biscuits and my emergency ration.

It was quiet, and I raised myself to the level of the trench and looked over. I could see two helmets protruding from a trench about thirty yards away. I called out, realising for the first time how painful my wound was now. Someone came doubling over to me after the second shout ; it was my batman. I asked him what was happening. Why hadn't the doctor and Battalion H.Q. come ? Had he any water ? He left me his bottle, and said he would collect my reserve one after he had gone over to the company commander to find out what was happening. He was a long time away, but finally returned with my bottle and a tin of German cold coffee. I drank it down greedily. He lay beside my trench and told me that the company commander was trying to get through to the Battalion H.Q. Apparently we were cut off and surrounded. He passed on a warning that the company commander was arranging for our artillery to break up a German concentration not far from our position ; it would be dangerously close shooting. A sniper started firing at him at this moment, and I told him to scram for his trench. He got there safely, but left his bottle behind.

Mortar shells started landing all around me. The Germans were watching our every movement, and had jumped to the conclusion that my trench was the H.Q. Twice I was covered in sand, and once a red-hot piece of metal landed on my chest. The Austrian stirred uneasily and woke up. He started to raise himself by placing his hands over the edge of the trench. There was an ear-splitting explosion. At first I thought our trench had been blown in. I looked carefully over the side; there was a huge crater less than five yards from the Austrian's end of the trench. Then I looked at the Austrian; he was lying half propped up against the trench looking curiously at the remains of his left hand; it had been partially blown away. I was nearly sick, but hastily tore my shirt and bound it tightly round the stump. He thanked me weakly and closed his eyes. His breathing was heavy and laboured; the poor devil was dying. I thought of his wife and children, of our talks about Austria, how damned stupid the whole thing was. First, he shoots me, then I shoot him, then we talk together as friends and share a trench where he is further wounded by his own side. Why were we fighting each other? Did it make sense? Then I thought of the massacres in Poland, France, Belgium. Yes, I suppose it was necessary. "Wann kommt der Arzt?" he interrupted my thoughts. Mechanically I replied, "Bald!" Almost petulantly he murmured, "Bald! Bald! immer bald." It was no use explaining to him that we were cut off and the doctor wouldn't be coming; he would certainly be dead in a few hours, and I, too, probably if this shelling went on. My thigh was hurting infernally. I tried to read a 'News Review' my wife had sent me, but I couldn't concentrate. I had put it into my haversack at the last moment, I remember, and had purposely left it unread for such an occasion as this, and now I didn't want to read it. I took out the photo I carried of my wife and children. How peaceful and unreal the house looked, how normal they all looked, but I didn't feel normal. I wondered if she was thinking of me at this moment; then my dream came back vividly—the bathroom—God! I was thirsty. I took another two mouthfuls of water. The Austrian stirred again and, opening his eyes, murmured, " Wasser bitte." Damn him! I thought. What was the use of giving my precious water to a dying man, and an enemy at that. I was angry. Damn him, hadn't he the sense to see that he was dying, and it would be just a waste of my precious water; but I leant over and held it to his mouth. He gulped it down, and when I tried to take it from him he struggled with me, hitting out with the stump of his bandaged hand. I felt guilty, but I forced it away from him; already he had drunk a quarter of a bottle.

As I moved back to my own end of the trench a bullet whistled past my head. That damned sniper was still watching. Our guns opened up now; the shells landed right among us. I hoped the wireless was still working, and the company commander would get through in time. Another salvo—just beyond us this time. I wondered how it would all end. I didn't really care much now. The subaltern I had argued with that night came doubling over towards me. I called out, and he shouted back, making a joke about the position of my wound. " I'm off to bring in our carriers; they are lost over there." He passed on—a bullet whistled after him. God, how strong the sun was!

There was the sound of explosions in the direction he had gone—grenades, I thought. I heard a faint shout, " Up the ——," and then silence. He never came back; his grave was found near Tobruk a few months later; he must have died in German hands.

The day dragged on; the shooting had died down, but it suddenly broke out again, but this time it was the sharp crack of tank guns. I appeared to be almost under their muzzles. A tank rumbled into view: one of ours—I shouted, but it was hopeless. The next moment it went partially over a trench in which some wounded, our own and Germans, were lying. I sank back into the trench. A little later an armoured car came up. I

## THE ATTACK IS RENEWED

shouted, and this time the officer inside heard me. He got out and doubled over to me. I shouted a warning to him about the sniper; he reached me and lay down beside my trench. He was amazed to find us there; they had no idea we were there. Apparently we were in the middle of a tank battle. I told him we had a lot of wounded; could he do anything to get us out. He said he would report it at once on his return to his H.Q.

It was now early evening. The Austrian was lying peaceful, still breathing, but blood was oozing out of his mouth. I think I slept again; I was getting light-headed. I finished the second water-bottle; my thirst was more painful than the wound. I still had my batman's half-full bottle, but I couldn't use that; he would want it. Another two hours passed, and then suddenly I realised there were people round the trench. I can't remember how many, but the company commander was there and a doctor, not our own. He was wearing a forage-cap, and I thought what a risk he was taking. He was very cool and cheery. "Hold out your arm," he said, and he injected me with morphia. I asked him to give some to the Austrian. He stabbed him, but he scarcely stirred, and murmured, "Der Arzt ist gekommen."

The doctor asked where the others were, and I pointed out the trenches I knew and called for my batman to guide him. Never have I seen such cool disregard for personal safety as that man showed. I don't know who he was; he strolled from trench to trench, completely ignoring the bullets and mortar shells which were hotting up again, his forage-cap stuck at a cheeky angle. Finally he returned to my trench unscathed. They held a hasty conference; I couldn't follow much, but I gathered that they were going to try and get the wounded out after dark. The Germans concentrated their mortars with increasing fury on my trench and the little party, which broke up hastily. I had an uncomfortable ten minutes, but I wasn't really caring at this stage. I had such a wonderful peaceful feeling. I must have fallen asleep again; for the next thing I remember, it was quite dark and men were carrying away the Austrian, who was apparently still alive. They came back for me, and pushed me on to the front of a 15-cwt. truck.

Soon we started off, bumping across the rough ground; one or two of the men inside groaned. I felt quite peaceful and had no pain. From time to time I had a feeling of anxiety in case I was going to be cheated out of my hospital bed at the last moment by a mine or a shell, but on the whole I was quite content to leave it to the driver.

We soon arrived at an advanced dressing station. I had another injection here, but after a quick glance at my bandage they left the wound alone. The last I saw of my Austrian he was lying on a raised stretcher having a blood transfusion. I wonder if he lived. I still have his papers.

I was placed in an ambulance, which was sheer luxury after the bumping of the truck, and soon we arrived at a big New Zealand casualty clearing station. They were frantically busy here, and when I assured them that I wasn't bleeding they just put another label round my neck and packed me back into another ambulance. From this I was transferred to a hospital train, and eventually landed at a South African base hospital in Egypt.

## CHAPTER VI.

### IN A SOUTH AFRICAN HOSPITAL.

IT was early in the morning of the 27th October when I was finally settled in the hospital bed. My wound had been cleaned and dressed, my blood-soaked shirt and shorts removed and burnt, and a kind and very gentle nurse, who spoke English with a strange guttural accent, had washed me down. I was clean, in a real bed, and safely out of danger. I gave a sigh of complete contentment and went sound asleep. It was about 4 A.M. the following day when I woke. I had slept without a break for twenty-two hours. At first I couldn't think where I was; then gradually full realisation of the events of the past few days came back I raised myself on my elbows and looked round curiously. I was in a large marquee with concrete walls. A dim electric light showed up the beds, fourteen in all, and every one occupied. Three beds along from me a young fair-haired lad was lying moaning quietly. A nurse was standing beside his bed adjusting a complicated leg-rest; another nurse who was sitting by the entrance got up and came over to me. I vaguely recognised her, and when she spoke I realised she was the same one who had attended to me on the previous day. " You have had a good sleep, skipper," she said. " Are you feeling better ? " It was the first time I had heard the term " skipper " given to an army captain. I was to hear it daily for the next month, for the South Africans addressed all captains by that title. I told her I was feeling fine, and asked if the wound was serious. She replied that I had had a miraculous escape, the bullet having just missed the bone and a main artery, but that I had lost a lot of blood and would have to take things easy. She gave me some Ovaltine, and then I went to sleep again. This time I had horrid dreams. I was to have them frequently for many months. I was back in the slit trench with the Austrian; he suddenly turned into the surly German officer whom I had interrogated. He was slowly emptying my water-bottle into the sand with a terrible sneer on his face. I tried to stop him, and just then the Germans attacked. I tried to lift a rifle, but he snatched it from me. The Germans came rushing in, and I awoke calling out loudly and with the perspiration pouring from my face. It was broad daylight and two nurses were standing over me, one holding my hand. " Take it easy, skipper; you're O.K.," said the latter. She spoke quietly and in perfect English without an accent. I realised I had made a fool of myself, and grinned feebly while apologising.

I felt very light-headed, and then I realised I hadn't had a proper meal since the night the attack started, just water, biscuits, a little bully beef, and the Ovaltine. The nurse must have guessed what I was thinking; for she said, " I expect you are hungry." I agreed enthusiastically and she went off, to return a quarter of an hour later with soup, poached eggs on toast, fruit salad and thick cream, coffee, and cream biscuits. I wolfed it all down and lay back completely at peace with the world.

After a few minutes I became curious to see who my companions were. In the next bed was a chap I recognised at once. He was a South African major who had commanded the company on my left when we first went into the line early in October. My patrols had come back through his positions occasionally, and we had had to make mutual arrangements. I saw that his right arm was in plaster up to the shoulder and he was obviously in pain. Rather diffidently I said, " Hullo, Major." He turned his head and said, " Feeling better ? I recognised you when you first came in. When did you get it ? " When did I get it—I had to stop and think; was this Tuesday or Wednesday. I asked him, and he said it was Wednesday afternoon. So I told him it must have been Sunday night. He was surprised when he learnt I had lain out over twenty-four hours before being taken back, that I was as fit as I was. He had got a burst of machine-gun bullets through his arm on the Saturday. His arm was shattered, but they were going to try and save it for him. On my right was a New Zealand captain with a bad head wound. They operated on him that day. One of my own battalion officers was opposite. He was an " up " patient, and another officer in our division was next to him. He had a slight wound on the nose which had already almost healed. These two were hardly ever in the ward and spent most of their time at the local officers' club, which was for the hospitals around. Next to them was a quiet dark chap wounded in the shoulder. I discovered he was a Maori. The young fellow who had been moaning in the night was a tank officer. He was to put up a grim fight for life. They tried to save his leg, but eventually had to amputate it. After the amputation he seemed better for the first two days, but he hadn't any reserve of strength to keep up the fight and passed away peacefully the third night after his operation.

The rest of the patients were all South Africans, who spoke Afrikaans to each other and English to the New Zealander and myself. With the exception of the major, they were inclined to keep very much to themselves, but never failed to ask how we were feeling, and when they received parcels from home they were very generous in sharing the cakes and puddings, &c., with us. Towards the end of my time in the hospital these parcels were mainly Christmas hampers, and contained a truly wonderful collection of rich food-stuffs.

One day a terrific argument arose among these South Africans. Tempers got a bit frayed and the atmosphere was very tense. I couldn't understand a word they said, but later that day I asked the major next to me what it had all been about. Apparently one had said that he thought there had been treachery on the part of a South African General at Tobruk and that this was the cause of the disastrous retreat. Others had indignantly denied this. The two sides were about equal, with a slight majority against the accusation. This argument had led to a bitter attack against General Smuts, whom one had accused of making repeated promises that they were going home. This had caused furious indignation with the Smuts' supporters, who were in a large majority. The major told me he had joined in at this stage and explained that it had been intended to send the South African Forces home, but the critical situation which developed during the summer had made a postponement of this plan inevitable. The major added that he very seldom joined in political arguments, because he was a " first generation " English South African, and nationalist feeling, though favourable towards the British war alliance, was inclined to be anti-British in home politics, and any criticism by a South African of English origin against Boer leaders was deeply resented. This interested me intensely, and when I was able to get up I went across to one of the most fervent of the nationalists and tried to draw him out, but he wouldn't play and quite politely gave me to understand that this was purely a South African affair.

After a fortnight I was getting on splendidly and was able to hobble about on sticks. I was being fed on a rich fat diet in order to counteract the effects of the loss of blood, and then I contracted jaundice. After two days of intermittent sickness I woke up to find myself yellow as a Chinese. My diet had to be completely reversed, and I was packed back to bed.

## CHAPTER VII.

### IN CAIRO.

It took me three weeks to throw off this complaint, and meanwhile my wound had completely healed.

After a little persuasion I got the doctors to agree to my leaving the hospital for a convalescent home, but there was a snag. The only kit I had with me was my washing kit, stockings, and boots. My only shirt and shorts had had to be destroyed. I had been going about in borrowed shirt and shorts, but the owner was now ready to get up himself and wanted these garments back. To make matters worse it was getting very cold, for it was now late November. I had sent for my valise, which had been left with the battalion stores before the battle, but I didn't hold out much hope of getting it; for the battalion was far too busy chasing Rommel across the desert to bother about me. Eventually I arranged with my friend in need to make the journey to Cairo, where I was going to convalesce at Lady Lampson's Officers' Home, and there I would purchase fresh kit and return the borrowed garments by mail. I arrived in Cairo with exactly 70 piastres (about 14s. 6d.) and presented myself—looking like a scarecrow—at the pay office; but when I explained that I hadn't my pay-book with me (one can't take these things into battle with one), I was met with the ultimatum: no book, no pay. I had already had to stand in a queue for three-quarters of an hour after a half-mile walk from the station, and I wasn't quite up to this sort of thing. I next went to the barracks and tried to draw essentials from the quartermaster's stores on a claim form, but they would not accept this unless signed by my commanding officer, who of course was far too busy some hundreds of miles away in the desert. I mention this to give the reader some idea of the impossible gulf which yawned between the fighting soldier and base red tape. I was far too tired and dispirited to continue the struggle, so made my way to the convalescent home in the suburbs of the town. I had to take a taxi out, and spent a heated five minutes arguing with the Arab driver, who had promptly doubled the fare registered on his meter. Finally, not without the help of my pistol, which I still hung on to, we came to an agreement, which reduced my worldly wealth to just over 7s.

The convalescent home was a large private house in charge of a lady housekeeper who was a character enough to justify description. I was greeted by a solemn dignified Sudanese, who ushered me into the " presence " with old-world ceremony. I introduced myself, and was inspected from head to foot in silence by a small elderly little lady with a sharp face, and, as I was to learn, a sharper tongue. Naturally I did not feel at my best in my meagre borrowed plumage; moreover, I was deadbeat, and my face and eyes particularly were still yellow from the jaundice. At last she broke the silence. " The hospital certainly did phone about you, but I had no idea when to expect you. I don't think I have a bed to spare. Why can't you people be more considerate and give adequate warning ; do you think this is an hotel ? "

She continued to scold until my heart sank to zero, and I prepared to pick up my haversack and get off ; where to I couldn't think. At this stage, realising that she had gone far enough in asserting her authority and independence, she ordered me to follow her, and led the way upstairs to a beautiful room where there were four beds, only one of which appeared to be occupied. She spoke again, this time in a less scolding, almost resigned voice. " Well, I suppose I can squeeze you in here." I thanked her very humbly and hastily put my haversack on a bed before she should change her mind. She then showed me the bathroom, sharply warning me against wasting water or making a mess, and then led me downstairs into a little office in the lower regions of the house. Here she started to take my particulars in a voice which would have done credit to any sergeant-major trying to impress a new recruit. " What is your name ? Spell it. Number ? Where have you come from ? Illness ? Oh, jaundice ; I can see it. They had no right to let you out of hospital in that condition." I interrupted at this stage to inform her that I was a battle casualty, and that the jaundice had only been thrown in for full measure. Her attitude softened immediately, and in a really sympathetic voice she asked for details. When I told her I was Scottish she became positively friendly and hurried through the rest of the formalities at twice the original speed. After she had finished these she gave me another good look-over and then remarked, " I don't need to ask where your kit and clothes are. You were evacuated from the field. When you were fit enough you wrote for your kit ; your unit probably sent it to the movement forwarding officer, and it has now probably been stolen by the Arabs. You can't buy any more because you haven't any money, and when you tried to draw pay you were refused because your book was naturally with your kit."

I thought this summary of my situation almost uncanny, and must have shown it, for she gave a short laugh and said, " You need not look surprised ; I am used to hearing this story by now. It would do some of those backyard boys good to experience a little active service, but they never will ; far too clever ! " I agreed fervently, for I was feeling rather sore at my recent treatment. Without another word she led me into a kind of laundry-room and fixed me out with a tolerably well-fitting suit of K.D. She then took me into the hall, and, with a return of her early sharpness, pointed to a notice-board on which the rules of the establishment were posted. Scarcely giving me time to read them, she barked, " Those rules *will* be obeyed, and if you are so much as one minute after 1 A.M. in returning you will find the outer gate locked ; the watchman has orders to open it to no one, and it is no use trying to climb in through the basement window, for I have had iron bars fitted." She looked at me in triumph as if to say, " That will stop your nonsense." I assured her I had no intentions of staying out late, that I had come here for a rest, but she interrupted me with, " Yes, yes, they all say that when they first come, but they all do it once." She dismissed me then, and I went up to my room, threw myself on the bed, and soon went to sleep. I was awakened by a Sudanese manservant, who informed me that it was time to dress for dinner, and looked meaningly at my shabby shirt and shorts. He was as majestic and superior in his attitude as any butler of an ancestral mansion in England or business magnate's villa in the United States.

He laid out my borrowed K.D. suit, and I started to change. I found I hadn't a tie, and he silently left the room without my saying a word and returned almost immediately with a perfectly pressed khaki tie. Shortly after, I went down to an excellently served and delicious dinner, and retired to bed almost immediately after the coffee, which was served in the lounge ! Thus I arrived in Cairo for my three weeks' convalescence.

The following morning I was awakened by the Sudanese servant about 8 o'clock. He solemnly handed me a cup of tea and a biscuit, and reminded me that breakfast was at 9 o'clock. Two of the other three beds were occupied, both occupants still being asleep. They were duly wakened and presented with tea. Both looked rather " morning after the night before," and I was soon to learn from them that they had only just " made the grade " in time. I was feeling much better, and viewed the struggles against officialdom which lay ahead of me almost with equanimity. After breakfast I sat out on the veranda for half an hour reading the ' Egyptian Mail.' The main news was the enemy's stand at El Agheila, the farthermost point reached in Auchinleck's 1941-1942 offensive. Was another Alamein brewing up ? The papers which a fortnight previously had waxed so enthusiastic about the American landings at Algiers, and which had headlined " Exciting race for Tripoli ! Who will get there first ? " had now toned down their original optimistic forecasts and were warning their readers that Tunis would not fall without a grim struggle. For the first time British units were being mentioned as constituting the main striking force of the 1st Army. At first there had been no mention of British troops at all.

About 10 o'clock I started to walk into town. I had known that it would be useless to start earlier, for working hours in military departments in Cairo were strictly limited. On arrival at the pay office I at once demanded to see the major in charge, and after initial hesitation I was shown into his office. He listened to my story with sympathy and attention, took my word for it that I had not drawn any pay in the previous month, and gave me authority to draw a full month's pay. He advised me to wait a little longer, and if my pay-book still didn't turn up I should return to him and he would issue me with a new one. If in the meantime I was short of cash I was not to hesitate to ask for him, and he would help me as far as was in his power. I thanked him, and as I left his office I compared the friendly helpful attitude of this " old hand pay-wallah " with that of his war-promoted assistants. With few exceptions I was to have the same experience throughout my service in Africa. Armed with the necessary authority I returned to the pay-subaltern, who silently paid out the sum asked for.

It is surprising how entirely different a city looks when you have a nice wad of notes in your wallet. The shops, taxis, entertainment advertisements, which half an hour ago had openly shouted their defiance at me, now seemed to welcome me with open arms. My next visit was to the bank, where, profiting from experience at the pay office, I asked to see the manager at once. I was shown into his office, and without more ado asked straight out if he would allow me to draw a cheque on my own bank through his. Though there was no connection between the two banks, and he had only my word that I had an account and that it was in credit, he agreed at once to advance me the sum I requested, and did not hesitate even when I had to ask him for a cheque. All I was asked for was my name, number, and regiment. I left the bank ready to face anything, and after a cup of coffee at Groppi's went on to the barracks. Following the previous successful procedure I demanded to see the officer in charge. After explaining my case to him he gave me a claim form, which I completed. I purchased the goods I required, and though I had to pay for them, he assured me that the sum would be refunded when my claim form had been duly endorsed by my commanding officer. I next went to Cook's and arranged for my service dress, which had been left in their Alexandria office, to be forwarded to Cairo. Well satisfied with my morning's work I returned to the home by taxi, and paid to the rogue who drove me three-quarters of the fare demanded. He gave me the pitying look usually reserved for greenhorns or those slightly inebriated.

After lunch I returned to the city and visited the movement forwarding officer. Here my formula didn't work; the officer in charge was *not* interested. I should have looked after my kit; I should have arranged for its return to Cairo if I was going to get wounded. It might come, but on the other hand it most probably wouldn't. I finally got a little help from a friendly staff sergeant, who, after painstakingly going through the names of kit-owners whose kit was " on the way," drew a blank, but promised to phone " up the line." Arranging to return on the morrow, and deliberately refraining from saluting the major in charge, I left, and spent the rest of the afternoon at the cinema, where I saw our own chaps entering Tobruk and a five-year-old film of American gangsters' life.

Returning to the home after dinner I found that two officers of my own division had arrived, and after dinner we went to the " Continental," where a good time was had by all. One of these officers was in the same boat as I over the kit question, and after I had given him an account of the day's experiences we decided to go out to Abbasia the following day, where the M.F.O. H.Q. was situated. We returned about midnight to find the little " warrior " woman still up. She gave us a sharp inspection, decided we weren't too intoxicated, and started to chat in a friendly manner. (I had learnt earlier that evening that my companions' experience had been much the same as mine when they first arrived.) The warrior told us that she had served as a nurse in the Boer War, in which we understood her husband had been killed, and during and after the last war she had organised relief in Greece and Yugoslavia, where her husband, presumably a second one, unless we had got the first part of the story wrong, was commanding a British force. She had later lived in India, and after a period of semi-retirement had volunteered again at the outbreak of the present struggle. Though we were never to lose our feeling of being like small boys caught in the larder by their governess, we came to admire her tremendously, and it was certainly the best-run convalescent home in the Middle East.

If there is another war in the 1960's I have no doubt whatever that she will be still " looking after the boys." These kind of people never die. The following day we travelled out to Abbasia by taxi, but the result failed to show any progress.

That afternoon, while coming out of the Continental, I was accosted by a tall, handsome Egyptian in flowing robes of an obviously expensive material. He greeted me with old-world dignity, and asked me if he could have the honour of showing me round his city. He explained that he was an official " Cook's " guide, and before the war had escorted most of the world's most famous personalities round the various sights. I was not particularly interested in buildings and monuments, but felt that I really ought to see the Pyramids, &c. I imagined how people at home would raise their eyebrows in pained astonishment if I had to tell them that, having spent three weeks in Cairo, I had not even given a passing glance at the Sphinx. Moreover, though not interested in buildings, I was intensely interested in people, and saw a chance of finding out first-hand how the Egyptian people really lived and what they thought about the war. In the short time I had been in Cairo I had already sensed the difference in attitude and atmosphere since my previous visit in August. There was a new note of respect, which even communicated itself down to the shoe-shine boys.

Thus I accepted his offer, and arranged to meet him the following morning at 9 o'clock at the Continental. I duly arrived at the appointed place a little after 9 o'clock, having had an early breakfast. My guide was awaiting me in the lounge; he was even more gorgeously dressed than on the previous afternoon, and greeted me with elaborate ceremony, which made me feel very self-conscious in front of all the people in the lounge. I saw some of the older ones smiling knowingly, while the younger ones clearly showed their contempt at this disgusting fraternising with a " Wog." However, having decided to go through with it, I assumed an air of complete in-difference, which was only shaken when my companion courteously took my arm and helped me down the steps, having noticed that I was lame. Outside, an elaborate " chariot "—no other word could describe it—was waiting, with an old Arab coachman polishing the already glittering harness of his horses. He bowed gravely on our approach and helped me up with elaborate ceremony. A small crowd of shoe-shine boys, picture post-card vendors, beggars, and hangers-on had gathered in the miraculous way they do in Cairo when they sense " wealth and power." At least six pairs of dirty brown hands struggled to close the low-cut door, and soon the whine of " Baksheesh, baksheesh ! " rose to a penetrating scream. Everyone on the hotel terrace, which was crowded, gazed with varying degrees of interest at the little scene, and a couple of dandies from G.H.Q. raised their eye-brows as they passed. By this time the crowd had grown to alarming proportions, and the chariot driver was swearing at the top of his voice—a particularly high-pitched one—while lashing out at everyone with his whip. I was beginning to regret my decision to go through with this ordeal, and to hide my confusion hastily dived into my pocket for my cigarettes. The packet was empty, and before I could prevent him my guide shot out of the gharry and disappeared into a tobacconist shop opposite. Immediately the crowd " cottoned on," and within seconds dozens of filthy hands were thrusting up at me, some whose owners were screaming for " falouse " with which to buy cigarettes for me ; others already thrusting grubby packets into my hands. Just as I was becoming desperate my guide reappeared and triumphantly presented me with a packet of the most expensive Egyptian cigarettes, which I detested. Hastily thanking him I suggested an immediate move, and, bowing slightly, he addressed the driver rather as I should imagine a Ruritanian Lord Chamberlain would address the Royal coachman. Followed by a screaming crowd of natives and the disgusted or amused looks of the Continental's patrons, we majestically moved off. I sank back and wiped my perspiring forehead. My guide turned to me and courteously asked me if I had any preference in the itinerary. I weakly murmured that I left it entirely to him, and soon we had left the busy modern main streets and were threading our way through narrow native quarters, dodging cows and barrows, and followed by a rapidly growing ragged crowd chanting, " Baksheesh, baksheesh ! "

When I had sufficiently recovered from my harrowing experience I realised that something would have to be done quickly about the obvious misunderstanding regarding my financial status. This ceremony, which I was supposed to be enjoying, would be costing me at least 10s. a minute. I hastily explained to my companion that I was a hard-up infantry captain, and must not be mistaken for a staff officer or one of his pre-war wealthy Americans. He answered gravely that he understood this perfectly, and that I should leave the financial side entirely to him. These wallahs, pointing to the driver's back, were all rogues and robbers, but he knew how to deal with them. He added that he felt it a great honour to escort a hero who had saved his beloved country from the wicked invader. This speech only alarmed me more than ever. I realised that the word " hero " would cost me at least a pound, and that his " protection " from the rogue and robber would be valued at another pound. The situation required immediate firm handling, and in the firmest voice I could muster I ordered him to stop the gharry, and, ignoring the gathering crowd, I said, " Now let's get this thing straight. I have exactly £3, which I am willing to spend on this expedition, and absolutely and finally *no more*. I expected him to look hurt or openly disgusted, but he just answered gravely, " As you wish, captain ; shall we proceed ? " Well, I thought, it is his own fault now if he finds himself out of pocket, so I replied, " Carry on." We stopped at the entrance to the bazaar, and, followed by our escort of beggars, vendors, and shoe-shiners, entered the dim passage-ways. I pointed out to him that I had already visited this place and wasn't impressed. He nodded gravely and carried on.

Soon we stopped in front of an oriental kind of chemist shop. Large and small highly ornamental bottles of scent filled every corner, and the strength of the various perfumes was nauseating. I hastily passed on, but he stopped me gently but firmly. " I wish to introduce you to a very old friend of mine ; you will find him very interesting," he said. Suspiciously I replied, " I am *not* buying any scent." " As you wish," he said. Doubtfully I followed him into the dim interior, gasping at the concentrated fury of the mixed perfumes. An ancient old Turk came forward, and my guide and he greeted each other in the elaborate Mohammedan manner. The Turk then turned to me and greeted me very courteously. " Welcome to my humble establishment, Captain. It is indeed a great honour you do me ; you who have so heroically fought and bled to save Islam." I moaned to myself ; another pound I thought. I thanked him for his kind welcome and admired his perfect scents. This was a fatal move. At once he produced three large bottles and, grabbing my arm, dabbed blobs of the contents on my sleeve. I stepped back in alarm and hastily rubbed the beastly stuff off. He seemed hurt and urged me to smell my sleeve. I did so hesitatingly and tried not to wince. I then assured him that I was not here to buy scent. At this juncture an assistant arrived with a tray containing the usual paraphernalia of Turkish coffee. The Turk poured out in silence and, with a deep bow, offered me a cup. Feeling that I was getting more and more involved every moment, I took the cup.

In an effort at leading the conversation off the sale of scent, I asked the Turk if I were correct in presuming he was in fact Turkish. He said he was, and so I continued by asking him what he thought of the war, and did he think Turkey would become involved. He thought for a moment in silence, and then replied: "It is the duty of all Islam to support the great British people in their brave struggle against the powers of evil. It would not be wise or helpful to your cause for my country to join you now in active warfare, but when the time is ripe we shall assuredly come in." He made his little speech slowly, obviously picking his words carefully, and somehow it did not quite ring true. Perhaps I was oversuspicious, but I thought I detected the scent-sale motif creeping in and influencing his reply. Perhaps I misjudged the man; I really do not know. I asked him what he thought the solution of the Arab problem was, particularly with regard to Palestine. He thought in silence again, and then replied: "It is necessary for all the Arab countries to come together. It was ordained that my country should be the leader, but our unfortunate and unnecessary participation in the last war put the clock back many years. It will take great statesmanship on the part of Britain, and understanding and tolerance on the part of the Arab world, to attain the conditions we all so earnestly desire. The Arabs in Palestine are mainly poor and ignorant; they fear the Jews will exploit them. In fact the Jews have already done so. Oil and water will not mix. Your great Lawrence understood; it appears there are few others who do. It is a tragedy.

I see no other solution than the complete expulsion of the Jews from Palestine."

" But surely," I said, " the Arabs who already own such vast areas could, in the cause of world peace and as a gesture of brotherly love, spare one small piece of land from their many ? "

" Yes," he replied, " that would have been possible twenty-five years ago, but now it is too late ; with British assistance the Jews have not waited for us to give them land to settle in, they have just taken it. The Arabs cannot forgive that, and only by starting from the very beginning can the harm be undone."

" But surely," I interrupted, " it was the Jews' own land they claimed back, and I believe, in most cases, paid for."

" That is certainly an argument worth consideration," he admitted, " but the Arabs look back further. The Jews robbed us of our own land in the first place, and we only paid them back in their own coin when we seized it back."

I saw we could go on with this indefinitely, and my guide was, for the first time, showing signs of impatience. I got up to go and thanked him for his hospitality, and told him I had enjoyed our conversation and would remember what he had said. Immediately he became the business man again, and I left the shop twenty minutes' later relieved of £3, 10s., for which I carried in exchange three small wooden bottles of allegedly rare scent.

We next crossed over to a modern-looking shop which appeared to deal mainly in brocades and tapestries. I shied like a frightened horse at the entrance and firmly said I was not going to buy anything else. My guide said solemnly, " As you wish, Captain. I now introduce you to a very good Jewish friend of mine. He is very honourable, and in his shop all prices are fixed and no bargaining is required."

" No," I said. " I take your word for his honesty, but I am *not* buying anything more."

" You are interested in our politics," he replied. " Is

it not only fair—cricket you would say—that you should hear the other side of your recent conversation?"

I succumbed to this bait and in we went. My guide introduced me to a swarthy Jew of probable Greek or Armenian origin. He was dressed in European clothes and differed little from those you may see in the business quarters of any of our big cities. My guide informed this fellow at once that I did not wish to buy, but that I was interested in local politics and wished to hear his views on the Palestine problem.

The Jew informed me that he was delighted, and, after arranging for an assistant to look after the shop, led us into a small office at the back, where the inevitable Turkish coffee was produced five minutes later. Meanwhile we started the discussion. I told him the Turk's views, without mentioning who he was, and asked him for his answer. He answered quietly at first, but gradually a note of excitement came into his speech. His main argument was based on the religious aspect. Jehovah had allotted that land to the Jewish nation for all time. He had led them through untold hardships to the promised land. The nation had claimed the land under Jehovah's direct orders, and had developed it and in it kept alive the germ of knowledge which was to blossom forth into our modern civilisation. The Jewish faith was the parent of all the world's faiths. Christianity owed its very existence to the Jewish Bible. Mohammed had been educated by a Jewish professor, who had taught him all he knew. The Jewish people had become slack and Jehovah had punished them, but He had never taken away their birthright; and then, suddenly switching over to the present time, he pointed out all the progress and modern industry and buildings which the Jews had introduced between the two wars into this disputed country. He claimed that the Arabs were a hundred times better off now than they had ever been, and that the Jewish immigrants had paid the Arabs handsomely for any land they had acquired. Before he had finished he was speaking passionately, as if his only task in the world was to convert me to his way of thinking. When he had finished the perspiration was standing out in beads on his face.

"Yes," I said, " I think you, too, have a very good case, but surely, even if you do get sole possession of Palestine, the majority of the Jewish people will never settle there ; their present businesses are far too profitable, and it is much easier for them to make money out of simple Europeans than out of each other."

" That is true to a certain extent," he admitted. " The persecutions, sufferings, and wanderings of generations have made us hard and sometimes unscrupulous, but with a land of our own to work for we would have an ideal, an object in life, finer and greater than mere money-making ; and though we might continue to live and trade in European countries, we should always look to our own country to pay back any profits we might make, by giving the world a new culture and new scientific wonders."

I wondered whether the rest of the world really wanted a new and Jewish culture, and whether it wouldn't be rather suspicious of such a bargain, but I refrained from saying so. I thanked him for his interesting talk and once more got up to go.

Half an hour later I left the shop. A large roll of brocade was on its way to my wife and a borrowed cheque for £16 was on its way to my bank.

I don't know how these fellows do it, but you just seem to walk out of their shops and find it has happened.

We walked along the bazaar, followed by shouting vendors of every conceivable article. I was pretty pensive, and my guide had realised, I think, that the limit in my sales resistance had been reached. At any rate he made no attempt to press me into any other shop and from time to time angrily shooed away the clamouring hangers-on. He confined himself to showing me a section of old wall, which quite easily might have been a portion of bombed London, and soon realising that I was not interested in architecture, old or modern, led me out of another entrance to the bazaar, where our gharry miraculously appeared at once.

I said I had had enough for the day and he instructed the driver to return to the Continental. I hastily asked to be let off at the bank, which was in a comparatively quiet street, and, thinking no doubt that I was about to replenish the purse, he gladly acquiesced. As we approached the bank he asked quietly, " What time would be convenient for you to meet me to-morrow, Captain ? "

I wasn't expecting this, and told him I was not considering another expedition.

" But," he said, " you have not seen the Pyramids or the great Mosque."

I agreed, but said they would have to wait for another time.

" The day after to-morrow ? " he suggested. " I have not earned my keep to-day ; my good friends will give me a handsome commission on their sales to you. I must repay your patience. I will take you, free of all charge, to the Pyramids to-morrow ; your only expense will be the taxi. Shall we say ten shillings ? Perhaps you can bring friends and then the expense can be shared."

I hesitated, and was lost.

" At nine o'clock, then, at the Continental, Captain," he said.

" No," I replied firmly and loudly, and gave him a rendezvous at the quiet end of the English Bridge.

He assisted me down, bowed, and I dived into the front entrance of the bank and, waiting long enough for the gharry to move off, slunk out again and made my way back to the home.

My friends asked me where I had been, and I answered vaguely, " Oh, looking round the bazaar ; not much to see ; and, by the way, I'm going out to the Pyramids to-morrow ; thought I had better have a squint at the damn things. Anyone coming ? " " Not likely," replied the others in unison. " Right-o," I said, and ordered a drink.

The next morning at nine o'clock I met my guide.

I think he was disappointed that I brought no companions, but he didn't remark on it. He had collected an ancient old taxi that coughed and spluttered along the wide main road, built for the convenience of rich peace-time tourists.

Our start and progress was as unostentatious as our start had been ostentatious on the previous day. I considered this a good augury, and, as far as the rather erratic movements of the ancient taxi allowed, I sat back and enjoyed the journey.

We soon arrived at a large square outside an hotel. Strung along the road as far as the eye could see were Arabs in charge of groups of dejected donkeys, still more dejected camels, and a few depressed and underfed horses. My companion called over an Arab who apparently owned two camels. He came over at a run, closely followed by half a dozen others, each claiming in " tourist English " that his particular beast was the only one fit to ride and the others were broken-legged and flea-infested. These accusations, if applied to all equally, did not seem far wrong. I asked the guide what he had in mind, and he informed me that it was a fair way to the Pyramids and we should have to cross the desert by camel. In alarm I said " How far ? " conjuring up visions of a day-and-night trek through the desert, stopping at the odd oasis for water.

" Oh, half a mile perhaps," my guide answered. Very relieved I said I would enjoy the walk.

" But you can't walk," he replied. " Nobody ever does."

" Well, I am going to," I said firmly, eyeing the leading camel with considerable distrust.

At that moment another Arab passed, leading a passable-looking white mare. I pointed to it and said, " I wouldn't mind riding that."

Three minutes' heated argument between the guide and the Arab, and the mare was mine for two hours for sixty piastres (12s.). Ignoring the kindly advice from my companion I jumped into the saddle and told him to lead on.

It was the first time I had been on a horse for two years, and I knew I should suffer afterwards, but I was going to enjoy this to the full. My guide had acquired a diminutive donkey, on which he sat side-saddle with his long legs touching the ground. Giving the beast a sharp kick in its belly with his heel he trotted off with me following at a dignified walk. The donkey had an amazing turn of speed, and I soon found it necessary to catch up. My mare thought otherwise, however, and nothing I could do would encourage her to break the majestic and dignified walk. Thus I arrived rather humiliated at the base of the first pyramid, which my guide had reached three minutes ahead of me. Dismounting, I turned the mare over to an attendant, paid my ten piastres, and entered the pyramid.

Small passages flanked by enormous blocks led into a cave-like room. Here an old Arab was squatting on the floor. Apparently it was part of the procedure to step on a certain flag-stone and have one's fortune told by this old villain. He scratched twice on the sandy floor making a rough St Andrew's Cross, and then, putting a grubby finger into the first section, reeled off in a monotone, " You have come from a far country to fight your enemies in the desert sands." This was pretty obvious, and didn't require much supernatural powers on his part. I agreed with him, as he apparently was waiting for it, and with a nod of satisfaction as if to say, " You see what powers I have," he transferred his grubby finger to the second section, and informed me that soon I would be fighting again, but that I should come through safely and eventually return to my family. " Sixty piastres, please." This was pretty quick work, I thought, and giving him five, passed on, followed by his curses.

On coming out into the open once more I duly admired and wondered at the pyramid as required by my guide. Personally I thought it was a much overrated and completely useless and unbeautiful pile of stones, not even geometrically perfect.

We then inspected the Sphinx, which was so surrounded

by sand-bags as a war-time protection that one could see very little of it. The next proposal was to visit another smaller pyramid which looked from the distance even less beautiful and symmetrical. However, it would be a pleasant ride if I could persuade my obstinate mount to trot.

We remounted, and immediately my beast seemed imbued with new life. Turning round, it started off at a smart trot in the opposite direction from that intended. I tried to pull her round, but her mouth was as hard as iron, and she made no response except to break into a gallop. I made another attempt to change direction, but finding this new activity very exhilarating I decided to give her her head, and off we went, streaking across open desert. After about half an hour we arrived at a well with a ditch leading from it; my beast immediately started to drink from this ditch. I didn't approve of this, for the beast was soaked in sweat from its burst of energy. The mare won the argument, and after satisfying her thirst, swung round and set off at a brisk trot towards the Pyramids again. I was relieved that we appeared to be in agreement at this stage, for I was getting a bit tired and I didn't care for the Arab-type saddle.

We finally arrived back at our starting-point, where the owner took possession of the beast without comment. I looked round for my guide, but he was nowhere to be seen. I sat down outside a small café, rather carefully, and ordered an iced beer. Half an hour later a very hot and worried guide rushed up to me and almost wept over me.

I had arranged with my guide, who had not breathed a word about payment for services rendered in his relief at finding me safe, to meet him again the following afternoon to complete my tour of inspection.

At 2 P.M. therefore we set off together in a gharry for the Citadel and the Mosque. It was a Friday, and when we arrived at the Mosque they were not very keen to let me enter, for it was their Sunday. However, my guide persuaded the doorkeeper, and, having taken off my shoes and donned a pair of bedroom slippers, we went in. A sprinkling of the devout were praying or listening to one of the most ancient men I have ever seen, who was chanting from the Koran. It was a spectacular but not beautiful building, with enormous glass or crystal chandeliers.

We inspected a few more ancient ruins, and then came the time for the great settlement. I thanked my guide for all he had done. He informed me that he had carried out his duties most unworthily and was not worth any recognition, and I, taking that as a hint and having completely failed in my fishing efforts to find out what it was customary to give him, presented him with an Egyptian pound and sixty piastres—about £1, 8s. He thanked me gravely and pocketed it in one of the folds of his garments, and at the same time produced a neat bill, headed by his name and description as an official guide. There were three items on it:—

To guide services on . . . £E.2
To supplying transport . . £E.2—60 piastres

and a small item for incidentals, which I remember included tips to Mosque doorkeeper and one packet of cigarettes. The total came to over £5. He informed me that he would be pleased to accept a cheque if I hadn't sufficient cash on me. I was completely nonplussed. I had half expected some bargaining, but this business-like account completely took the wind out of my sails. I feebly murmured something about the sum I had just given him and started to deduct it from the bill, but he stopped me politely and gravely, pointing out that the bill he had presented was purely a business matter and had nothing to do with my expression of appreciation, for which he was exceedingly grateful. I made one more attempt at reminding him that I had warned him that I was not prepared to spend more than £3, and that he himself had told me his services were amply repaid by the commission he had received on my purchases. He gravely informed me that he had already allowed for that. I gave it up and forked out. He thanked me formally and wished me good luck and disappeared, leaving me to pay off the gharry. I wasn't really angry; it was impossible to be so. I shrugged my shoulders and made for my pay-office major.

The next few days I joined up with my fellow officers; they pulled my leg about my mysterious behaviour during the past three days, but I remained discreetly silent on these experiences.

We used to go to Groppi's every morning for "elevenses," which usually consisted of a massive fruit salad, ice-cream sundae, and cream cakes. We elected ourselves as honorary members of Groppi's Light Horse, as we called the hard core of "Permanents" who minced in (it is the only word to describe their mode of entry) every morning at the same time and remained talking loudly until it was time to adjourn to the Continental Bar. At first we discussed them frequently with disgust, but as the days passed we got used to them and scarcely noticed them, except occasionally later on at night when one or two of them attempted to be rude, usually about our dress. They were then given more attention than they desired, and after a few nights their manners improved noticeably.

I was still attempting to trace my lost kit, and eventually I recovered a valise which contained one boot, one puttee, a sock, a torn shirt, and someone else's wife's photo. An Italian sergeant's tunic was thrown in for full measure. On further inquiry I learnt that the kit had been sent back from Tobruk by the battalion, together with other kit. It had been left unguarded in a railway siding at El Daba for two days by the local M.F.O. During this time the Arabs had helped themselves to everything of value, a total of over £40 worth of kit, in addition to personal belongings, including a valuable gold watch which had been a present to me. I inquired about compensation, and was informed that as the kit was not destroyed by enemy action I could not claim on it. I was further informed that the loss was due to my own carelessness. I reported the M.F.O. for negligence of duty, but nothing came of it; and it was only much later, when my commanding officer took the matter up, that my claim was eventually allowed to the value of £2, 0s. 4d. in cash and approximately £4 in kind. The £2, 0s. 4d. has not yet been paid!

The days passed rapidly. Nearly every day we rowed across the Nile to the Gezira Club. There was a small Arab urchin who always claimed us as his special fares. My friend, who was large and very fierce-looking, used to do the bargaining with this child, and every day it was the same procedure. The child would demand five piastres (1s.), and my friend would reply "Two." The child would grin. We would get in; half-way across the child would ask for his five piastres; my friend would promise to give him two at the end of the journey. The child would turn on the tears like turning on a tap and would howl at the top of his voice. I would say, "For God's sake give him the five." The child would turn off the tears just as abruptly. My friend would give him three, the tears were renewed, but he recommenced to row. A continual switch from tears to smiles would go on for the rest of the journey, the child holding out for his five piastres, my friend pretending to get angry and finally giving him the five. Both we and the child derived considerable amusement from this daily act. Incidentally the same journey before the war would have cost half a piastre, five piastres being sufficient to keep an Arab family for a week. That child must have earned about £7 a week.

On the last Sunday before our convalescent leave expired I went to the service at the Church of England cathedral. On seating myself I looked round with interest to find out what the congregation of a mixed city like Cairo would consist of. It might have been the congregation of any wealthy West End church. Retired officials, diplomats, civil servants, a sprinkling of khaki represented by G.H.Q., and a very few men in battle-dress.

The service was dull and uninspiring. It was a good choir, but it had caught the mood of the congregation, " Let's get it over as soon as possible ; we must come ; it is expected of us ; we have always done so, as our fathers did before us." The preacher was an Anglican Bishop from England. I listened with interest to what message he had to give to this dull and super-respectable congregation. It started with an appeal for money for some obscure charity ; it continued on this theme in a dull, monotonous voice. Apparently the speaker did not really believe in the needs of this obscure cause, but he had to put it over ; the congregation expected it. After all, they might as well know what they had to fork out for—or did they want to know ? I don't suppose more than ten per cent knew the title of the cause at the end. The sermon ended with a few general platitudes on charity, and the congregation rose with relief to sing the last hymn with their minds on their conventional English Sunday lunch. I wandered out ; nobody said good morning, and I made my way back to the home for my English Sunday lunch.

That evening I decided to peep into a Methodist church. I had heard from some of the boys that they had a very nice welcome at the church canteen. I arrived just as the service was starting. The church was packed with soldiers, Air Force men, and A.T.S. Everyone sang the cheerful well-known hymns as if they meant it. The minister preached a simple message on faith. It was very simple but very genuine. After the service he stood at the door and shook hands with the congregation. He told the soldiers and A.T.S. that the canteen was open and that there was to be a sing-song. I pondered rather deeply as I strolled back over the Nile. Each church catered for what its members expected, I supposed. I am not a member of any special church.

Two days later I was reporting to the infantry depot for posting back to my unit.

## CHAPTER VIII.

AT THE INFANTRY TRAINING DEPOT AND UP THE LINE.

ON arrival at the depot I met several officers of my unit who, like myself, had been wounded, and were now waiting to go up the line again. The authorities had just started an energetic "hardening course," which every officer, whether newly out or returning to unit, had to pass through before being posted. I am sure it was an excellent idea, but I knew quite well that my thigh would not yet stand up to this sort of thing, and moreover, owing probably to the rich food which I had been eating to excess in Cairo, and even more probably to one or two nights of drinking at the Continental, I was suffering from a return dose of jaundice. Fortunately it was the Christmas week-end and a two-day holiday had been announced, so the problem was solved for me at least for the first three days, as Sunday was also treated as a holiday. On Christmas Day there was a compulsory church parade, held in the local cinema. What could have been a really cheerful and satisfying service turned out to be a dreary repetition of the cathedral service in Cairo. The few carols we did sing were almost unknown to us, a meaningless lesson was read from the Old Testament and the sermon consisted of a series of mixed platitudes, and only a vague passing reference was made to the Christmas message. What a chance was missed to put over a real Christian message to this crowded congregation! for it consisted of men who would shortly be once more engaged in bitter fighting, and for many of whom this was to be their last Christmas. There are many good conscientious padres in the Army—our own unit's one was a good example—but so often it seemed to me that those who have the greatest opportunity to meet and influence the largest number fail miserably in their task by their hide-bound devotion to strict orthodoxy or, even worse, through sheer laziness and indifference.

Christmas Day was a depressing day. As it was a Scottish Mess, the special dinner was being reserved for New Year's Day, which we were to spend in a transit camp that had already consumed its special fare at Christmas! There was no mail, and owing to the effects of the jaundice I was unable to join in the revelry round the bar in the evening. Three days later we were on the first stage of our journey back.

It was early on the 28th December that we entrained at the depot sidings. There were about forty officers and three hundred other ranks. We were packed tightly into cattle trucks, which were none too clean, and there we remained—standing room only—for the next four hours, finally arriving at Amarya Transit Camp. This camp was one of the original transit camps that had been made in the early part of the war. We lived eight to a bell-tent, and fed in a semi-permanent Mess with ante-room and bar. For a camp so long established it was not well run. We paid $2\frac{1}{2}$ piastres (6d.) for dinner and a further $1\frac{1}{2}$ piastres for breakfast. Our return for this outlay was about half of our entitlement of normal free army rations, and a very occasional " extra " in the form of a sweet. The bar, too, was badly stocked and indifferently run. One expects this sort of state in the forward areas, but there is no excuse for it in a base camp settlement situated within easy reach of Alexandria, with a large permanent staff. We spent two days here and then moved into Alexandria, where we embarked in an ex-Canadian Pacific liner converted into a troop-ship.

Most of the officers were junior subalterns on their way up for the first time, so I had little difficulty in acquiring one of the best cabins on the ship, and was far more comfortable than on our voyage out from Britain. We sailed almost immediately, escorted by two ancient French destroyers (not from the French Fleet at Alexandria, which at this time had not yet joined the Allies). These destroyers were so slow that we had to reduce speed in order that they might keep up with us. I enjoyed that trip in the Mediterranean : a trip which in peacetime would have cost at least forty guineas. We had only one minor submarine scare, and on the afternoon of New Year's Eve, 1942, sailed into Benghazi harbour, or rather came as near as we could. As we approached the town it appeared to be quite untouched by war. The white walls and coloured roofs of the houses stood out against the green background of the palm trees and cultivated fields, and the large gilded dome of the cathedral looked particularly impressive ; but we were to be disappointed when we landed. Owing to the number of half-sunk ships—German, Italian, and British—lying in the harbour, we had to land from barges on the much-bombed mole. The pillars of triumph—erected, I believe, in honour of Mussolini's last visit—were still in position, standing rather forlornly at the entrance to the badly cratered but still beautiful promenade. The modern houses and hotels which stretched along the sea front, and which from the sea had appeared quite undamaged, now proved to be little more than empty shells.

We embussed as soon as transport was available, and drove about two miles out of the town to the transit camp. This was situated in a park which had once contained the local zoo. The animals' cages were still intact with their name-plates attached, but there was no sign of the animals themselves. The Officers' Mess was in a road-house, tents being provided in the garden for the officers to sleep in. It took us the rest of the day to get settled in, and when the bar opened we decided to celebrate the New Year in camp and postponed our sight-seeing trip to the town until the following day. Unfortunately a N.A.A.F.I. ship had been hit by German bombs in the harbour two days before, and supplies were therefore very limited, and consisted only of one can of beer and three mugs of local wine. The bar closed at about 9 P.M., and after talking for a few minutes longer we decided to go to bed, and so for the first time since I was a child I did not " see the New Year in." At about

1 A.M., however, we were awakened by the sound of heavy firing and the explosion of bombs, and came out of our tents to watch a wonderful display of fireworks. During the week I was at Benghazi the harbour was raided every night but one.

The following morning we walked into the town. It was terribly battered about, and completely deserted except for local Arabs and British troops. The Royal Engineers were already on the job blowing up dangerous buildings and fixing telephone wires. There were no shops open, but there was an Arab market of sorts where a nondescript crowd of Arabs and Jews sold useless trinkets and souvenirs from barrows. These consisted mainly of stores pillaged from the local schools—exercise books, pencils, pens, history books illustrated plentifully with pictures of Mussolini's triumphs. German and Italian badges and medals and picture post-cards, the latter having a brisk sale among the troops who strolled around.

I tried to buy a fountain-pen, but having no Italian money and being unable to spare cigarettes—the international currency—I failed. We next visited the cathedral, which, apart from a few holes in the roof, probably caused by shrapnel, was quite untouched. There was a service in progress, so we did not stay. I noticed that the congregation consisted mainly of British troops, with a slight sprinkling of Italians. There must have been some of the local Italians left, therefore, though we never saw any in the streets, and there was scarcely a house fit to live in. Returning to camp for lunch, we were informed that there would not be a convoy leaving for two days at least. There was nothing to do in the camp: no books, and only the doubtful pleasure of drinking the local wine—a particularly sour brew—from our enamel mugs, and even this was rationed to one and a half mugs per day. The camp staff had made a real effort to create a semblance of comfort, and, working under far more difficult conditions than at Amarya, they succeeded in producing quite attractive improvised meals from the

Army rations and a few local products. No charge was made for this, the cost being met from the profit on the bar.

The following morning I walked into the town on my own, the others being busy washing clothes. I inspected a large hotel on the promenade, and discovered the shattered remains of what had been once a very fine wine-cellar. The spilt wine had run all over the floors, and had soaked into piles of copies of a German Army newspaper. There also I found a copy of the Afrika Korps song, " Lili Marlene." I inspected the cathedral more thoroughly : it was a modern building, simple and austerely beautiful, and had only been completed in the middle 'twenties. On my way back to the camp I passed a pretty villa which had escaped the bombs, and in the garden a small fair-haired boy of about ten years was playing with a toy horse. It was the first European child I had seen since leaving home, with the exception of the children in Cairo Cathedral. He and the toy were so out of place in this devastated town that I stopped. He looked up and smiled at me, and said, " Buon Giorne." I replied, and he came over the garden wall and said, " Inglese ? " " Scotsezi," I replied. This puzzled him, and making signs to me to wait, he dashed into the house shouting at the top of his voice. An elderly man dressed in white drills came out and greeted me politely in English. I replied, but found that his English ended at " Good day." I tried French, and he replied at once, but his French, like mine, was weak, and conversation was difficult. I next tried German, and found his German about the same as his French. By a judicious mixture of both we got on quite well. He told me he was a doctor, and had lived in Benghazi for eighteen years. He had volunteered to stay behind when the authorities decided to evacuate the Italian population. His wife and two daughters had returned to Italy ; his eldest son was in the Army, and he had not heard from him since the previous October when he had been at Tobruk. His youngest child, the boy I had seen, had been seriously ill at the time of the evacuation and had had to be left behind. He told me he had once visited Liverpool when he was a ship's surgeon during the last war. It had been cold and wet, and he was appalled at the filth and squalor and the dirty black buildings. He had heard of Scotland. The south had been colonised by the English, had it not? and there was a famous medical university at Edinburgh where the native children were taught to be doctors. The rest of Scotland, he thought, was wild and inhabited by a semi-savage race rather like the Albanians, who wore strange robes. From time to time the English Government had to send punitive expeditions against these people, as his own Government did against the Albanians.

I thought at first he was pulling my leg, but realised later that his knowledge of all affairs outside local medical practice was extraordinarily limited. He was not even quite sure which side the Tedescis (Germans) were on, and had a muddled impression that we and they were fighting against each other and that the Italians were trying to keep both out of their country. He was nearer the truth in this than he realised! He had heard, and had every reason to believe, that Mussolini was a great and good leader who had saved his country from being overrun by the French. He had once lived in Savoy, and it was there that he had learnt to speak French. Recently the authorities had insisted on his learning German. He had tried hard, but he was too old to learn anything now, and he had so much work to do in the town, especially since all this dreadful bombing. Why did the Inglese want to destroy his lovely peaceful town? Could they not fight their battles in the desert if they really had to fight at all? The Germans had told him, and his son who had attended the local school also told him, that the English were fighting to steal his town because they were jealous of all the great achievements that Mussolini had effected in colonisation. He supposed the English would be leaving again shortly. As far as he remembered they usually left towards the end of January. This was always a disturbing period, and created more work than ever for him, and to make it more difficult the Germans always insisted on his working part-time in their military hospital. When he had first come to Benghazi the town had been rife with typhus and malaria. Before the war, after many years of hard work and persuasion to get the authorities to lay proper drains, he had almost succeeded in eliminating both diseases, and now all his work had been wasted and disease was rampart, and in addition he now had all the bomb-injured people. What savages the English and the Germans were!

I had listened with interest and amusement to this outburst, which had taken a considerable time and had been energetically driven home by many gesticulations. The little man stood there perspiring freely from his efforts. I tried to explain to him that it was Mussolini who had declared war on Britain when we were almost defeated, that we did not wish to fight the Italians, and that we didn't want his town. We were only there to drive the Germans out, and as his countrymen had joined the Germans they would have to suffer too. I don't think he tried to understand this; he shrugged his shoulders angrily and replied, " If you were nearly defeated you should have given in and saved all this unnecessary bloodshed." If Mussolini really had declared war on England, it was because he wanted to convince her that it was wicked and useless to continue fighting. If we had been sensible his work wouldn't have been disturbed; but when he remembered how cold and depressing Liverpool had been he could understand us wanting to steal his beautiful Benghazi. I gave up and asked him about his work. He waxed enthusiastic about this, and told me, among other things, that he had reduced the mortality rate among the local Arabs from 120 per thousand to under 70. At this stage he broke into another outburst against the Inglese for interrupting his work. After accepting a glass of wine, I left him. I saw him several times during the next few days; he was rushing from house to house with his little boy, sometimes stopping to inspect a blown-up drain as he passed along the street. This strange little man, with his hazy views of the war and its causes, lived only for his great work of healing.

That night I had a more violent recurrence of the jaundice which had been hanging about me, and the next morning I was feeling so ill that I decided not to accompany the others who were moving off by convoy " up the line." I went to see the camp medical officer, and he advised me to rest and diet for a week. I did this for five days, but it was difficult to diet in a transit camp where the bulk of the meals consisted of army rations which are normally designed to give abundance of fat. At first I was rather lonely and wished I had gone on with the others, but the Mess soon filled up again. The worst thing was the complete lack of anything to read.

During these days I was to be asked several times by Arab egg-vendors and the like, " When are the Inglese leaving again ? " Already they were becoming impatient, and the street barrows were beginning to show English souvenirs in preparation for the expected return of the Germans, which during the past two years had occurred about this time, and which the Arabs had no reason to suppose wouldn't happen again. When I told them we were intending to stay this time, they were incredulous or quite angry at the thought of the seasonal loss in trade.

Among the new arrivals in the Mess was a young Jewish second lieutenant whose uniform and kit looked startlingly new. He was bubbling over with enthusiasm about everything, and told everyone, whether they cared to listen or not, that he was going to be attached to a Palestine Army service petrol unit. He had been called up in England and chosen for this job because of his knowledge of Yiddish. That evening he was tackled by a young infantry officer, who asked him why it was that there were so few British Jews in the British Army and, in particular, in fighting units. I listened with interest to this conversation, for the same thing had often struck me. The little Jew looked rather distressed, and at first tried to convince his audience that in proportion to their numbers there were as many Jews as British in the Army. This was not allowed by the interested party which had gathered round to listen. The Jew then admitted that there were very few actually in fighting units, but his race was not warlike and, on the whole, did not make good soldiers, and he maintained that it was better, therefore, to face facts and that they should serve where they could be of most use. He gave examples of Jews in charge of supply depots, civilian and army catering establishments, institutes, and he admitted that he himself would be useless in a fight, but was willing to work night and day if necessary to supply the front with all its requirements. Someone mentioned the large number of Jews whose names were appearing in connection with black-market charges at home, and someone else said he thought that the Jews would have been glad of the opportunity to get their own back on the Nazis by actually fighting them.

There was a complete lack of rancour in the arguments, and the little Jew answered good-naturedly, admitting that many Jews were involved in the black market and how ashamed he was of them. He stuck to his guns about serving where they could be of most use. I suggested that the Jews surely had quite a warlike tradition in the old days and quoted the incident of David and Goliath. He flashed back right away, " Yes, in those days we could fight it out as man to man, and we had a country to fight for, but since then we have suffered generations of persecution, and, being deprived of the means of defending ourselves and being always in the minority, we have learned other and more subtle means of fighting for our existence. Unscrupulous ones among us use this ' sixth sense ' for their own selfish ends and give our whole race a bad name. It is these men who cause hatred of our race in so many countries in Europe. Our wits, also, have been sharpened by centuries of precarious existence, and this sharpness now makes us successful in trade, and this again causes jealousy and hatred."

I kept an open mind on the issue, but I admired that

little Jew for his good-humoured reasoning and defence of his race, and particularly for his admission of their faults. He helped his people's cause greatly that night, and I could see that even his chief " accuser " was impressed by his plucky defence.

Eight days after my arrival I left Benghazi, travelling on the top of large barrels of petrol in a convoy of about eighty trucks. The convoy was only going about sixty miles up, and after that my fate was in the hands of the gods. I had no idea where my unit was, but the front had moved up beyond Sirte, which the wireless had announced had been captured two or three days previously.

There were four of us " going up." A South African doctor, two officers from my own division, and myself. A large party of R.A.S.C. officers, including the little Jew, had left the previous afternoon by special truck. As we skirted the harbour of Benghazi I noticed that a large convoy had arrived. The sea round the harbour was dotted with ships of all sizes and types.

Apart from the smell of petrol we were quite comfortable on top of the barrels. We had opened our valises and lay full length with our heads propped up against the driver's cabin. At first the countryside was unspoilt except for signs of hastily deserted camps in the groves. We passed a prisoner-of-war camp where two months ago the present guards—Indians—had been the prisoners. Along the road there were frequent warnings to keep dispersed because of danger of air attack. Some of these warnings were arrestingly grim. By the remains of a blown-up truck there would be a single grave with a simple wooden cross. Beside it there would be a large notice with an arrow pointing at the grave. The legend read, " Do you want to join him ? He didn't keep his distance between vehicles ; are you ? " Another frequent warning was, " 'Ware mines," again a lone grave, and the notice with arrow. " He pulled in for a ' brew up.' It was his last ! " And again warnings against speeding. " Dangerous bomb-craters ahead ; slow down ; the boys up there need your load urgently." Again the grave,

## AT INFANTRY TRAINING DEPOT AND UP THE LINE 87

notice, and arrow. " This chap tried to pass here, now he has passed over." None of these notices, grim though they were, was meant to be taken as " cheap humour " : they were simple statements intended only to save lives by constantly bringing home to the drivers that they were not on the Manchester-London run.

Yet in spite of all these warnings we travelled nose to tail in one long line stretching back as far as one could see. There were two explanations for this. First, the front had been pushed forward a further hundred miles in the last few days, and the danger from air attack had lessened. Secondly, there was so much going up and the need for speed in delivery was so great that risks had to be taken. One of the main factors contributing to the Eighth Army's thousand-mile advance was the efficient organisation of the supply lines and the gruelling hard work of the Royal Army Service Corps drivers, some of whom lived and slept in their trucks for weeks on end, driving a hundred miles or more a day without rest, and only one who has seen the conditions these fellows had to drive under can understand what that meant. If some of our workers at home who were going out on strike on the least pretext could have realised what these fellows were doing, I think the most hardened of them would have been ashamed. It was a cause of continual irritation and bewilderment that these strikes were tolerated by the folks at home, and no one out there spared words in expressing their disgust.

We stopped in a siding for a " brew up " and " tiffin " about mid-day. Everyone mucked in together, pooling rations as required. The inevitable " Wogs " appeared from nowhere, and we exchanged our used tea-leaves with them for eggs. I am not quite sure whether these " Wogs " smoked or boiled up the tea-leaves again, but once when one of our chaps gave one of them some fresh tea-leaves he returned later, indignantly asserting that he had been cheated and that we had given him dried leaves from the trees.

We drove on again until an hour before dusk, and then

handed in our tins of meat and vegetables to the self-appointed cook, and sat round yarning till the stew was ready. The evenings were still cold, and as we sat round our petrol-and-sand fire with our blankets draped round us and our cap comforters over our heads and faces, we looked very like the wandering Arab families who passed us from time to time.

These drivers were nearly all old hands, and could tell stirring stories of Wavell's and Auchinleck's pushes and the subsequent retreats. They all had a tremendous admiration for the " fighting boys," and considered their life an easy one in comparison. Though they certainly had the advantage of being in constant touch with N.A.A.F.I. supplies, papers, &c., and didn't suffer the dangers and hardships of the battlefield, they lived a life that made the home worker's long day's work followed by the night at home with the wife seem like a pre-war holiday at Blackpool. They had their grouses, of course. Lack of mail from home was the chief one, so often they were away from their bases for several weeks, and had to wait until they could return before collecting their mail; but when they heard that the last letter I had received was dated early in November they were full of sympathy.

We slept that night inside the trucks with their hoods up. We had got used to the smell of petrol, and preferred it to the icy wind blowing across the desert. The next afternoon we arrived at the supply dump just east of the Cyrenaican-Tripolitanian border, where Mussolini had erected a triumphal arch which our boys had promptly nicknamed " Marble Arch." Marble Arch had figured prominently in the news during the previous campaign, being the farthermost area reached by our troops. I examined it curiously, and thought how typically it illustrated the petty vainglorious ambitions of its builders. The long straight road ran mile after mile through the completely desolate desert, and passed through this huge useless monument to continue its dreary way as far as the eye could see. Early that afternoon we had passed through the battlefields of El Agheila, where Rommel had attempted to make a stand. The desert on both sides was littered with broken guns, tanks, masses of barbed-wire, and well-dug positions still intact. Tattered bits of garments clung to strands of barbed-wire, helmets—German, Italian, and British—lay about with rusting rifles, piles of mines cleared from the roadside were stacked waiting shipment back. We passed graves, sometimes single, with a rough cross or British or German helmet on top. Once we passed a large German cemetery with rows of well-made Maltese crosses, among which plain British-type crosses were interspersed. Some of these graves had elaborate stone designs and edgings and long inscriptions; others contained only the barest details of the dead soldier's name and number.

We stopped that night in a temporary transit camp attached to the supply depot. I made inquiries from a Stragglers' Post (small posts set up at intervals along the lines of communications and manned by military police, who were kept up to date, when possible, with the locations of units). Here they told me that my division was some eighty miles on, but they thought it was on the move. The South African doctor left us here, having discovered that his unit was some sixty miles back. He was an elderly man and took life very seriously. While we were content to lie back and let the trucks take us wherever they were going, he was constantly consulting his map and shouting instructions to the drivers, who took not the slightest notice of him. He kept ordering them to stop so that he could make inquiries from a control policeman, who of course had no information. After two or three of these stops, our driver got " browned off " and said he wouldn't stop again for anyone or anything. Every time we stopped we held up the traffic for miles and miles back, and within two minutes there was a bedlam of indignant hooting from the impatient drivers. We were all glad to see this officer go; he had got on our nerves with his continual depressing prophecies that we were irretrievably lost, and that soon we would run into the enemy lines.

Our convoy was not going any farther, and the transit camp commandant said we should have to make our own arrangements unless we liked to wait on the chance of a reinforcement convoy coming in. We spent the night there, and the next morning helped each other to carry our kits down to the roadside, where we stood thumbing trucks. Soon a 15-cwt. truck drew up and a convoy of 3-tonners filled with tins of petrol drew up behind it. I went forward and asked if they could give us a lift; to my surprise the little Jew I had talked to at Benghazi popped out and welcomed me warmly. He was going up another hundred miles, though not necessarily on our sector, wherever that was. He proudly told me he had been given immediate command of a petrol transport unit on reporting, and this was his first assignment. He was to go right up to Advance Army H.Q., and perhaps farther. Did I think he would see any action? He was anxious in case he was dive-bombed; but his anxiety, I think, was mainly on behalf of his load. He was bubbling over with enthusiasm, but was quite relieved when I gravely assured him that he would not be likely to experience any action as far back as Army H.Q., or even Divisional H.Q., with the possible exception of an odd divebomber. We piled in our kit, taking a 3-tonner each, and this time, as the English-type petrol tins couldn't stand our weight, we sat in front beside the drivers.

The programme of the previous days was repeated. We stopped for " tiffin," and again in the evening. The Palestinian drivers could not speak English, and our little Jew was our only interpreter. They produced a wonderful evening meal and refused to accept our rations. We slept on the ground. It was bitterly cold, and we slept uneasily. The ground was very rocky, and we only had two blankets each. I had no greatcoat.

We were up at first light, mainly, I think, because of the little Jew's enthusiasm. We made a feeble attempt to shave in an icy wind with driving rain. In spite of the weather the Palestinians produced a wonderful breakfast with real Scots' porridge or a very good substitute. We climbed into our cabins and started off just as a watery sun was coming out. Soon it was intensely hot; what with the heat from the engine and the powerful rays of the sun, we sat and perspired. The road, which until then had been first-class, if narrow, now became little more than a cart-track.

There were few signs of fighting, only a few discarded trucks, an occasional helmet, and track signs, German and British. We passed a few more graves at the side of the road; one had an elaborately carved white crucifix and was edged with white stones, in the middle was a large bunch of dead " desert daisies." I would have liked to stop to see who this was who apparently was held in such esteem by his fellow soldiers.

Soon we began to see the first signs that we were approaching an operation area. First, Army H.Q. signs, then Corps H.Q., then we saw our own divisional sign. The convoy had stopped while our little Jew was making inquiries at a Stragglers' Post. I walked over and inquired where our division was; the military police informed me that it was some twenty miles back. We held a quick counsel of war to decide what we should do, and decided to stick with the convoy until we reached a H.Q. where we could arrange transport back. We drove on a further twenty miles, where we arrived at a forward supply depot. Here we learnt that most of our division had passed through a few hours ago, and that my brigade had been right forward for three days. Somewhere beyond Sirte, he thought. We stopped the night there.

Here I first sampled the salt-marsh well water that we were to exist on for the next week. I thought at first that someone had put salt in my tea instead of sugar, and I remarked on it. The R.A.S.C. officers laughed and told me that I would have to get used to it. It was not only salty, but was sickly as well. It was almost undrinkable as water, but boiled with sugar one could just drink it as tea. We slept the night at this depot, and the following morning they lent us a truck to take us up to our own brigade supply point. Here we met our respective quartermasters and parted company. I heard all the latest news of the battalion during the remainder of the journey. Something was brewing, and it appeared that we were about to go into battle. Meanwhile we were holding a reserve position west of Sirte and about five miles from the enemy lines.

To my surprise I learnt that the others who had left Benghazi five days before me had only just arrived that morning. Apparently they had caught the division in the process of moving and had been directed to the main divisional area from which our brigade had been detached.

I had arrived back early in the afternoon of 12th January 1943, and sensed at once the suppressed tension and activity that precedes " going into action." The commanding officer welcomed me and asked me to take over a different company from my old one. He told me that we were moving forward for the attack the following night. We were bombed and machine-gunned that afternoon, and I realised that I was really back in it for the second round.

## CHAPTER IX.

#### FROM SIRTE TO TRIPOLI.

THE following morning I attended a conference of all divisional officers down to company commanders. It was held near the beach, a large-scale model of the battle-plan having been designed on the sand. Here at Sirte, as before at Alamein, no trouble was spared to put us all in the picture down to the smallest detail. Although some measures had been taken against possible air attack, I could not help thinking, as I gazed round the crowd of officers, all keenly studying the sand-map in front of them, what a devastating blow the enemy could strike at this moment by dropping one bomb in the middle of this assembly of all the commanders great and small of the force about to strike them. However, enemy planes kept away, and soon we were back with our units. There was a vast number of preparations to make, and I was somewhat hampered in this by not knowing any of my key men in the company, with the exception of one officer. I did not know on whom I could rely and who required supervision; moreover, I was feeling far from well; the jaundice was still persistently hanging round me, and the many hours of travelling had made me unused to walking and standing about for long periods.

The following morning company commanders with a skeleton force took up positions just behind the mobile screen we had previously thrown out to keep contact with the enemy. Our battalion rôle was to be the firm base through which the attack would be made. It was a rough and difficult journey up, working round wadis, bumping across rocky desert, and avoiding the soft patches of sand in which our company trucks could get so easily bogged. On arrival we were shown our positions, and company commanders went off to do their reconnoitring. The main body was to come up under cover of darkness and we were to meet them at a given point at 10 P.M. that night.

The time passed quickly and soon we were on our way to the rendezvous. The rendezvous had appeared prominent and unmistakable by daylight, and after memorising its features and general direction I had not bothered to take a compass bearing, a sure sign that I was out of practice in active service conditions, and had already forgotten the lessons painfully learnt in the pre-Alamein days. I started out confidently enough, but after half an hour I had still failed to find the R.V. It was ridiculous : my Company H.Q. was less than half a mile from it, but after dark the desert plays strange tricks on objects which are quite prominent by day and even stranger tricks on one's bump of locality, never a very strong point with me. I passed through ack-ack and machine-gun positions, but so indifferent is the ordinary soldier to anyone outside his own particular formation, that I was unable to get any help from them. Fortunately I had allowed myself an hour to get there, and when three-quarters of an hour had passed I decided that the only thing to do was to go back to the H.Q. and start all over again ; for by this time I had hopelessly lost my direction. This was not too easy either, and it took me half an hour and a good deal of wandering about before I found my own H.Q. I started off once more, pushing forward anxiously ; for I imagined my company standing about impatiently waiting for me.

This time, by hard concentration, I found the R.V., though I walked right across it once without realising it. No one had arrived, and the other officers were sound asleep in hastily scooped-out " beds " in the sand. That accounted for my not having heard any sounds or seen anyone during my previous wanderings. I discovered, to my disgust, that one of the ack-ack posts where I had stopped to inquire during my first journey out was less than fifty yards from the R.V. I had walked about four miles in all for the best part of two hours.

I settled down like the others and tried to get a little sleep, but I had left my coat behind (a coat drawn from the company store on my arrival) the second time I had started out because I was too warm; now I began to get colder and colder. I lay there shivering for two hours before the first troops arrived. They had had a terrible journey across the wadis, frequently losing their way or getting bogged down in the soft sand. They were in troop-carriers driven by Indians, and the inability of these Indians to understand the orders and directions given to them by the guides and officers in command vehicles had caused frequent misunderstandings. Two did not arrive till the following morning. My company arrived, however, and eventually about 4 A.M. I had them all settled into their positions. We were up again within three hours for stand-to. This was the first of ten nights during which I was not to get more than two hours' sleep in any night. There was another conference that morning; apparently the enemy had pulled back to their main positions during the night and we were going to push our firm base forward a further three miles or so.

During the afternoon I had an opportunity to explain to the men what was happening. Monty had issued his famous message, " Tripoli in ten days." We were all rather incredulous about this, but I put it over to the men with all the conviction I could muster, and such is the make-up of the ordinary Jock that what they wouldn't take from the " heid yins " they would accept with absolute faith from an officer they knew, though most of these chaps only knew me by name and from what they had heard from friends in my old company.

Just before dark the major, who had led the company at Alamein, returned from the front, where he had been in command of the special mobile force, and took over. Although the distance across country to the wadi we were to occupy was not much more than three miles, we had to get to it by a long circuitous march, working in and out of wadis with so many bewildering turns that the best of us lost all sense of direction. Once we had to turn back and march past groups of gunners who were busy preparing their evening meal. We had passed them going the other way half an hour previously, and even then it had been difficult to prevent some of the men from breaking ranks to cadge a mug of tea or soup. This time it took all the persuasion of the officers and N.C.O.s to maintain march discipline, and I breathed a sigh of relief when we were finally past. We were dead-beat and footsore by the time we arrived. Part of the way the going had been across terribly rough stony desert. The stones cut into our boots and made us stumble, laden with kit as we were.

The company commander left me to place the company and went off to Battalion H.Q. We could hear the guns firing, and the flashes lit up the desolate ground in front of us. Machine-guns, ours and theirs, rattled unceasingly on our left. I ordered the platoons to dig in quickly in the areas I had allotted, and started to reconnoitre for a suitable Company H.Q. I had scarcely started when a loud explosion came from the direction of the platoon I had just left. There was some mortaring going on, and I thought they must have given their positions away to the enemy. This idea was strengthened when a moment later a further four explosions occurred in the same area.

I went across to see what was happening, and found five men badly wounded and three killed. Among the wounded was the platoon sergeant, who was also platoon commander. Sending a man back for the company stretcher-bearers, I lifted the sergeant and started carrying him back to Company H.Q. There was a further explosion behind me as I started off. Half-way back I met the stretcher-bearers, and ordered them to bring in the rest of the wounded. I had had to stop for a rest twice on the way, for the sergeant was heavy. The stretcher-bearers went on, and I started to lift the sergeant once more. Just then there was another explosion just behind me, and I saw the stretcher-bearers fall. It was then that I realised we were in the middle of a concentration of anti-personnel mines. A cold shiver ran down my spine as I realised I had not only walked right through it, but had walked about in it while trying to patch up the sergeant and during the rests *en route*. It was hopeless to try and look for them in the dark, and the only thing to do was to carry on and trust to luck. It was a nightmare of a struggle back. The sergeant got heavier and heavier, and every step I took I expected to be my last. As I approached H.Q. someone came out to help me, but I shouted to him to stop where he was; the more people moving about, the more chance there was of standing on a mine.

I finally got my burden safely in, and immediately issued an order to everyone to stand where he was and not move. I had to find out how far the mines extended. I had left orders with the platoon which I had just left to pick up kit and come in to Company H.Q., thinking at the time that they were being mortared and I should have to find a fresh position for them. It was too late to stop them, and the only thing left was to hope for the best. They arrived shortly, carrying in four wounded and four dead men. By good fortune they had not stood on any more mines.

Having organised a mine-searching party to clear the area round Company H.Q., I decided that I should have to get through to the platoon beyond the minefield in order to warn them not to send men back until a path was cleared. No one except myself knew where they were, so there was nothing for it but to double back across the mined area myself. Crossing my fingers for luck I started back, and, passing one of the stretcher-bearers on the way, I stopped only long enough to discover he was dead, and arrived safely at the platoon. The platoon commander had realised what had happened. He had actually been on his way to Company H.Q. when the first mines exploded, and had rightly decided that it was no use taking unnecessary risks, and had returned to organise a mine sweep of his own platoon area.

Once more I had to face that nightmare journey back. The problem was whether to crawl slowly feeling for the mine-prongs, or just to dash across and trust to luck. I decided on the second alternative, and bounded across, keeping as much as possible to the same route as before. I got through safely, and after seeing the last of the wounded temporarily patched up and evacuated to Battalion H.Q., Company H.Q. dug in, and the mined platoon settled in new positions, I turned in in the trench dug for me and my batman, who was already asleep in it. We were up early for stand-to the next morning; it had been after four o'clock before I had turned in and I felt dead tired. We had breakfast of bully and biscuits, washed down by half-cold tea made from the salt-marsh water. It was so filthy that I decided to shave in it instead, and drank a little of the water from my bottle in which I had placed two saccharine tablets to counteract the saltiness. The attack was supposed to go in at 3 P.M. that afternoon, but 3 P.M. came and went without any sign of action. I slept fitfully from time to time, but there was much administrative work to be done, and I was feeling too tired to sleep.

In the afternoon two signallers passed through our area followed by a carrier. I warned them of the mines, but they carried on, and a few minutes later there was another explosion and one of them returned to say that his companion had been killed. We got the body in, and the padre came up a little later and held a burial service for all the killed, representatives of all companies parading round the graves. Our company sergeant-major had made rough crosses, and we placed one at the head of each grave. It was an impressive service, and somehow we all felt the death of those chaps more than we had felt the death of far greater numbers at Alamein. I think this was because it had not happened in the heat of battle, when one has not time to realise death, let alone having the opportunity to give a decent burial.

In the evening we heard that the attack had been postponed until 10 P.M. Shortly before 10 P.M. we stood ready waiting for the sound of small-arms firing which would let us know that the attack was going in, but the silence was unbroken except for the occasional sound of a heavy gun. Almost at 10 P.M. word came through that we were to prepare to move. At first we thought it meant that we were to put in the attack, but when troop-carriers arrived up we heard that the enemy had pulled out and that we were to give chase. We embussed about midnight and moved off about two hours later; first of all, trucks following each other nose to tail, and then, as we came out on to the open desert, we opened to eight columns, well spaced out. Other battalions were doing the same, and as far as the eye could see the flat desert was covered with the fast moving dots behind which clouds of sand and dust were swirling in the air. The advance to Tripoli had really begun.

All that day we tore across the desert, trucks heated up and radiators boiled over. Occasionally a truck got stuck in soft sand, another would stop and pull it out, and both would race forward again over the rough desert until they had regained their positions in the column. Sometimes a truck broke down altogether, and the occupants piled into another truck already loaded to capacity. The broken-down truck was left to be salvaged later by the Brigade Light Aid Detachments (R.E.M.E.), which were following up at a slower pace. Once or twice a truck was blown up on odd mines, but we soon left the minefields behind.

Mile upon mile the desert stretched, and, as far as the eye could see, in all directions were trucks of all sizes and types tearing across the desert with only one purpose in mind—to catch the enemy. We slept, as far as we could sleep, in the trucks. Relief drivers took over, and throughout the night we carried on at only slightly reduced speed. Rations were doled out in the trucks as they sped along, and the first stop was for breakfast after a day and night of continuous travelling. Petrol was running low, and more and more trucks were dropping out. We halted for about four hours, and during that time many trucks which had dropped out struggled in with engines coughing and spluttering. A petrol supply column came racing up, and dashed from vehicle to vehicle filling up empty tanks. Company commanders' 15-cwt. trucks fussed around collecting the sections of their companies like a hen collecting her chickens. Then we were off again, racing madly on towards the sea and the coast road.

Early that evening we saw the first signs of cultivation far away in front of us. Gradually we could distinguish little white farmhouses surrounded by cultivated fields and trees. We were coming up to one of Mussolini's much advertised State-owned farm colonies. Now we could see the Mediterranean bright blue in contrast to the yellow sand and green fields, and beside it the coast road winding towards the town of Homs, built beside the site of the old Roman town of Leptis Magna. Civilisation again, and probably thousands of enemy troops between it and us.

We camped the night, the second since the advance proper had started, by a little Arab farm on the edge of the cultivated coastal strip. The Arabs came out to stare in amazement at the first British troops they had seen. They told us with much enthusiasm that the hated Italians were well beyond Homs, having raced through that town the previous day, leaving vast stores behind in their haste to get away. They sold us eggs and a whole sheep, which we killed and ate right away, roasted or rather grilled on an improvised grill.

We were no sooner settled in, however, than word came for us to move on again, and tumbling sleepily into our trucks we moved on until we reached the main road. Here we found a huge crater where a bridge had been blown up, and we were told to set-to and fill it in. We worked all night in shifts, but as there were only two officers we had practically no sleep between working our shift, feeding arrangements, and general supervision. In the morning we moved on again, stopping from time to time to fill in more craters. That evening we worked again in shifts on a particularly large crater, and then shortly after midnight we moved forward part of the way by truck and part on foot to the outskirts of Homs. By this time I was able to sleep every time I sat down, and, like an automaton, got up again when we moved on.

We took up positions on high ground overlooking Homs. The enemy were shelling us in a desultory way, and it was almost dawn before we were settled in. I made my H.Q. in a large dug-out, but had scarcely dropped off to sleep before an officer came round warning us that we were not to interfere with the excavations of the old Roman ruins. I was very angry at being disturbed for what appeared to me a quite unimportant matter, and even more annoyed when the officer informed me that my present abode was an " excavation " and I should have to move out and dig another. I knew little about excavations of ancient buildings, but I could recognise an enemy gun-site when I saw it, and that was what I was in at the moment. The " excavation " was so new that the grass had not yet pushed its way through the sand which had been thrown out at the top, and the ground around was littered with shell-cases. For the sake of discipline and the preservation of " ancient monuments " I had to move out, and had hardly settled in to another hole before the order came to move.

The company commander had gone forward the night before and I was now to march the company through the town, which had fallen the previous day, to high ground adjoining the coast on the other side of the town. It was growing hot as the morning advanced, and soon we were roasted as we dragged our tired bodies through the town and across the sand-dunes. The enemy was still on the high ground to our left, and we could see the flashes of his guns, but he made no attempt to hinder us.

We arrived on the high ground about noon and started to prepare our breakfast, which there had been no time to have before starting. The water for the tea was almost boiling when the order came to move on again. We poured the tea into the hot water and drank it as it was. The tins of bully had been already opened, and knowing that they wouldn't keep I allowed the men to eat as they fell in and moved off. We marched or rather stumbled on the whole of that day. The idea was to go across country and cut off the enemy in the rear where our path would strike the main road. The going was terrible, stumbling up one long ridge only to find on reaching the top that there was another just as formidable in front. Every time we halted we fell asleep where we sat, but the other officer and I had to force ourselves to wake half-way through the ten minutes' halt and spend the remaining five minutes shaking the men into some sort of consciousness. That march will always be a nightmare to me. Already five nights had gone by since I had had any real sleep. I was weak from the jaundice and out of training after my time in hospital and convalescent home, and the stiff climbing was affecting my wound and causing my whole thigh and leg to throb.

We arrived by the road just as it was growing dark; not a man in the company had fallen out, though some were struggling on half a mile behind. My company had been leading, and by the time the rest of the battalion had closed in I had had half an hour's sleep. The company commander rejoined us and told us that we were going forward to ambush the road immediately. I could hardly get my body to respond to my will, but was in the process of reorganising the platoons when he came up to me and said, "I am leaving you behind at Company H.Q. with a few men. Take up an all-round defensive position so that we can fall back into prepared positions if we are attacked in strength." I am afraid I showed my relief, for he looked at me and said, "You look all out." I tried to grin, and made some stupid remark like, "There's still life in the old body." The ambushing party went forward, and, after preparing the defensive position, I posted sentries and went to sleep. I felt no qualms of conscience at leaving an N.C.O. in charge; for, apart from the fact that he had had more sleep than I during the past five nights, I knew that I would have to be fresh to take over when the main body returned.

I must have slept for two hours when I was awakened by the sentry shaking me and telling me that someone was approaching. I had lain down where I was on the ground, and now I was shivering all over; for I had been perspiring freely and now I was soaked in night dew and a cold wind was blowing in from the sea. With my teeth chattering I went round with the N.C.O. turning everyone out. It was difficult to wake those dog-tired men. We stood-to and waited till I heard the pre-arranged signal and knew it was our own men returning. I went out to meet them, and learnt that they had arrived in time to see the tail-end of the enemy column disappearing down the road towards Tripoli, and a few minutes later the head of our armoured column arriving. There had nearly been a disaster; for in the dark our men had mistaken the armoured cars for Germans and were just about to open fire when they realised their error. It was decided to move on to the roadside and await orders and our transport.

Our commanding officer had gone off the morning before on a reconnaissance and had not been heard of since, and our second-in-command, who had led us across the hills, was becoming anxious, particularly as news was coming through of a stiff battle that had been fought by another battalion in our brigade which had made its way later in the day along the coast. It was in that direction that our C.O. had gone. Rumours spread that he had been captured. We lay down by the roadside, but it was so cold that, tired though we were, we could not sleep. A jeep came up with two war correspondents; one of them kindly lent me his valise and blankets and slept in the jeep himself. I got another half-hour's sleep before I heard the excited voice of our divisional commander. It was decided that we should attack a hill on the left of the road from which the enemy had been shelling us. We called this hill " Edinburgh Castle "; for there was some sort of buildings on the top of rugged cliffs which closely resembled it.

We had an early breakfast, and another battalion which had come up by road made the initial attack. This was not altogether successful, though the enemy pulled out of their lower defences. An hour before our attack was due to go in, word came back that the enemy had pulled out. Within seconds, it seemed, troop-carriers and trucks of all descriptions poured along the road. We piled in, and off we went again, tearing down the road as hard as we could after the retreating enemy.

Passing through a small village we saw signs of street fighting; bodies were lying about on the roadside. We pushed on till we came to a part where the road ran parallel to the coast, cut deeply into the side of the hill. Here the enemy had blown the road up, and it had collapsed down the steep cliffs on to the beach below. This was a serious block; already engineers were at work, and soon bulldozers came up and dug their way into the hillside to make a circuit round the crater. We joined in and dug the earth out of the hillside and threw it into a part of the crater where the road had not completely collapsed. Soon the first truck was able to pass precariously across with its nearside wheels only a few inches from the crater's edge and a sheer drop down to the beach below. Round the next bend was a similar crater, and there were two more farther on. Although we got trucks through fairly soon, it was not strong enough for the tanks, and the work went on all the rest of that day and night. Gradually we were able to filter the heavy vehicles through, but after each one we had to rebuild the road before allowing the next one to come on. About midnight we were relieved and marched back a mile to a rest area. We were told that we were to get at least seven hours' sleep, but had hardly got between the blankets, which had been brought up with the rations, before the order came through to get up and get back to the trucks. We sat in the trucks for nearly an hour, and then received another order to de-bus and prepare to advance on foot. We started marching about 3 A.M. and marched steadily till 9 A.M. For the first time men fell out; but what I think contributed to this was that empty trucks were passing us going forward and covering us with sand and dust as they rushed past. Behind us, too, other trucks and troop-carriers were trundling along in low gear consuming twice as much petrol as if they had picked us up and driven on at normal speed. I don't know whether " someone had blundered " or if there was an explanation for this, but it made the officers and N.C.O.s' job twice as hard as it had been during the gruelling march across country.

We finally arrived at a blown-up bridge and there captured a very dirty German. He said his truck had broken down, but I suspected he had been left behind to blow the bridge and his pals had driven off without him, for there was no sign of a truck. There was no way of repairing the bridge and we had to find a way round. We started to make a road leading down into the river-bed, which was fortunately almost dry, and soon trucks and guns were swaying and slipping down the steep banks and tugging and heaving their way up the other side.

For the first time we were short of rations. Our quartermaster had performed miracles in finding the companies, scattered as we were over miles of ground during the past six days; but this time we had outstripped him and we had to make do with what was left. One company was given permission to eat their emergency ration, but we made do with remnants, and then, having arranged working shifts, the rest of us went to sleep. Within two hours we were on the move again with orders to proceed to the next block, but when we were ready to move off the order was countermanded and we camped in a wood on the far side of the blown-up bridge.

The company commander and I went off to reconnoitre for water and eggs. We found an Arab farm with a modern well; it had been recently used as an Italian H.Q. The half-Arab, half-Italian owners were friendly and drew water for us. After making them drink some first, we filled our bottles and returned to the camp to organise bottle-filling for the company. I exchanged my last packet of cigarettes for some eggs, and we had quite a good early supper. We went to bed about 9 P.M., but we had no blankets or greatcoats and it was bitterly cold. I couldn't sleep. About 11 P.M. I heard trucks arriving and went out to meet them; it was the " B " echelon trucks with blankets and rations. We doled out both and settled down to sleep again, but for the fifth night running we had hardly closed our eyes before the order came through to prepare to move. Up we got again. We only had the 15-cwt. truck and the " B " echelon 3-tonner which we were sharing with another company. The company commander decided to go on with the 15-cwt. and the 3-tonner, emptied of all unessential stores, which were dumped at the roadside. Every man possible was piled in, and the rest of the company was left under my command with orders to bring it up by any means possible to the first road-block which hadn't got a working party.

After the two company trucks had gone, I organised the rest of the company into parties of six and waited at the roadside. Every vehicle that passed I thumbed vigorously. Some stopped and others didn't. Most of them were already crowded with men and stores, but I got men on somewhere, clinging to gun-barrels, sides of tanks, on roofs of drivers' hoods, astride water-wagons, every conceivable vehicle imaginable. I was lucky to get a lift on the bonnet of a 15-cwt. truck. We drove on through the dawn mist almost frozen stiff. We passed several road-blocks, but they all had working parties, so we didn't stop. I wondered if I should ever get the company together again. I saw with a thrill a signpost saying " Tripoli, 18 kms.," and wondered if we should have to fight our way into the town.

About 12 kms. from Tripoli I saw the company commander standing at the roadside. He had already collected those of the company who had gone on ahead of me, and by the time I arrived we had about two-thirds of the total. The remainder had an officer with them, so we decided to push on again. Our orders had been to advance until we found a road-block without a working party, and we had not yet found one. The traffic was thinning out now, and we drove the next six kms. without seeing a single vehicle. Already there were signs that we were approaching a large town. Petrol stations, large villas, and farms. Huge vehicle dumps and stores. The road widened into a first-class carriage-way, and then we came to a fork. There was no signpost and we stopped to consider where we were. We had long since run off the maps we were carrying, and the only thing to guide us was a map of Tripoli on the wall of a nearby garage. Two trucks full of Jocks from another battalion passed us, and we decided to push on and catch them up; for we wanted to be first into the town. There was no sign of the enemy; even the road-blocks were not in position. We drove on and soon came to wide modern streets. They were completely deserted except for a few Arabs, who eyed us curiously, but did not respond to our shouting. The Jocks had been asleep in the trucks—we had left the rest to come on as best they could—but were now wide awake and cheered every time they saw a garage or cinema or other buildings which showed them that they were back to civilisation.

Thus we drove into the main square of the town. Here a remarkable scene met our eyes. The square was packed with tanks and armoured cars, and trucks were disgorging crowds of dirty, weary troops. The divisional commander raced up to us in a jeep. " What are you doing here ! " he shouted. " Your battalion is a hundred miles back. Good, anyway, we can make use of you; go and take over the radio station and get out of here quickly; there is enough congestion already." Off we went again, trundling round the town trying to find the wireless station. Another brass-hat stopped us and told us to throw a cordon round a big square and not allow anyone through.

I made my H.Q. at a small café and paraded the men I had left, thirty of the dirtiest, scruffiest gang I had ever seen. I was wearing a lance-corporal's greatcoat and had two days' growth of beard ! In spite of the strict orders we had in the division to shave whatever the circumstances, it had been quite impossible during the last forty-eight hours. Just then an Italian policeman, dressed in the most immaculate uniform, with spurs and jackboots and gaudy epaulettes, came up and gave me a flourishing Fascist salute. One of the Jocks asked grimly if he should " stick him," and advanced threateningly with his bayonet fixed. I stopped him, and the policeman asked me something. The only word I caught was " officiale," and guessing that he was asking for an officer, I pointed to myself. The company commander had gone off to consult the divisional commander, and I explained by signs that I was the senior officer present. He looked incredulous and eyed my dirty appearance with surprise and a little disgust. I demanded impatiently what he wanted, and when he finally understood, replied in a torrent of words from which I finally gathered that he wanted to hand over to me. I followed him to a police station where he showed me a lot of papers and orders which meant nothing to me, but I gathered that the Army had moved out two days previously, leaving the police in charge. I was to learn later that the Arabs had immediately gone wild and had looted and pillaged the town, not even sparing the cathedral. During these two days the police had locked themselves in their stations and left the citizens, who had not been evacuated, to their fate.

I returned to my temporary H.Q. and found a meal ready. The men were busy washing and shaving, and I followed their example. After breakfast and washing I posted sentries, and the rest of the men stood about watching the scene curiously. An excited woman came up jabbering at a sentry, who was trying to push her away. He brought her over, and she chattered away at me with much gesticulating. I couldn't understand a word, and I shook my head. She tugged at my arm and seemed to want me to follow her. I couldn't leave the H.Q., so I shook her off. Just then an old man came out of a bakery opposite, and she screamed to him. He came over, and after she had chattered to him for a while he asked me in good French if I spoke French. I replied, and he then explained in a bored voice that the woman had run a brothel for the German and Italian soldiers, and she would like to offer her services to me, and would I honour her by accompanying her to inspect the premises and inmates. All the time he was speaking the woman was tugging at my sleeve and nodding her head vigorously while shouting, " Bon ! bon ! bon ! " I burst out laughing. I had thought that at least her house had been attacked by Arabs. Anything less desirable than a brothel run by this dirty old hag I could not imagine. A good sleep and a square meal were the limits of our desires at that time. I shook my head and told her to go away. She screamed at me for a few minutes, and then tossing her head she cried, " Inglesi, bah ! " and spat on the ground. A Jock standing by enjoying all this pretended to load his rifle and pointed it at her. She screamed and ran off as hard as she could. We all laughed and then carried on with our washing.

A little later we moved into the wireless station, which had been completely destroyed except for the actual buildings. Beautiful modern transmitters had been ruthlessly smashed up, and I could scarcely bear to look at the awful waste as I wandered round the control rooms. Throughout the day the remainder of the company dribbled in, and by 6 P.M. we had all but two accounted for. Thus we arrived in Tripoli, nine days after we had left our camp beyond Sirte and eight days from the time the advance actually began. We had beaten Monty's time-schedule with a day in hand.

## CHAPTER X.

### RESTING IN TRIPOLI.

TRIPOLI was a great disappointment to us when we eventually found time to explore it. For a night and a day after our arrival we did little more than sleep. The battalion gradually filtered in, and after two days our "B" echelon arrived with what food-stuff our quartermaster had managed to collect *en route*. We moved from our billets in the radio station to a camp just outside the town. The weather was cold and wet, and our bivies could not stand up to the heavy rains. The food question was serious, for Army supplies had been left well behind in the hectic chase. We fared better than most battalions; for our quartermaster had somehow or other managed to bring quite a large supply with him. The Germans and Italians had taken almost everything with them, and anything they had been forced to leave behind had been pillaged by the Arabs before our arrival.

It was not till the third morning after our arrival that one or two of us set off to explore the town. What we had seen on our way through had appeared quite promising, and now we expected to find all the shops open again and picture-houses in full swing. We found the European part of the town still shuttered up and no form of entertainments laid on. The only goods that could be purchased were worthless trinkets which the Arabs were selling from barrows, also a few doubtful sweets and little "pokes" of monkey-nuts. We wandered disconsolately about, as hundreds of others were doing. We heard that there was an officers' club in the "Grand Hotel," and we went there. The hotel was untouched by the war, and an attempt had been made to get it working normally. Water and electric light were not yet restored, but if one brought down one's ration of bully and tinned potatoes the hotel staff was willing to cook it and serve it up in a luxurious dining-room for a reasonably small sum. We went back to camp and collected our rations and bought a few eggs and vegetables on the way, and after handing them in to the maitre d'hotel we adjourned to the bar, where there was a choice of three rather sickly sweet wines and a wishy-washy local brew of brandy. The dinner was quite successful. We had soup made from a tin of Maconochie's, omelettes, sliced bully, boiled potatoes and vegetables, and one portion of pear each from a tin that one of the officers had brought with him from Cairo. We washed it down with a bottle of white wine each. The bar closed early on orders from the military authorities, so we returned to the camp.

The military authorities had issued special occupation money—£1 notes, 10s., 5s., 2s. 6d., and 1s. notes—and these were on a rate of exchange of 400 lire to the £. This made the lire worth approximately a halfpenny, and it would have been a very satisfactory rate for us if there had been anything to buy and if the authorities had made any attempt to prevent the inflation which set in immediately. We used lire for small change, and within a day of this new currency being introduced all the small change had miraculously disappeared, and at the same time the price of every article, however worthless, was based on 1s. and multiples of 1s. Thus six monkey-nuts wrapped in a piece of newspaper were " una sheeling." Tins of boot polish stolen from German and Italian supply dumps rocketed from two for 1s. to one for 2s.

The authorities made no attempt to stop this racket, except to advise the troops not to spend their money; but although this was the first time for at least six months that the troops had had an opportunity to spend their pay, a big " smarten-up " campaign had been started, and articles like boot polish were essentials. We tried to save the troops from being exploited by buying the boot polish in bulk. I went myself into a small shop owned by an Italian Jew and told him that I wanted three hundred tins, but it was no use bargaining because

I was not going to pay more than 6d. a tin. He went out and got them from a friend's store, and I handed over the cash. Immediately he started screaming that the price was one for 2s. and that I had swindled him. So little respect had they for us already that he cursed and swore at me. I felt like shooting him on the spot, but fetched two military policemen instead. They started to take him away on my instructions, and all the bombast went out of him and he whimpered that he would return me half the price if I let him go. It was fortunate for me that he did not call my bluff, for the authorities at that time would not have taken him in charge. Later an attempt was made to stamp out this terrible abuse, but the harm was done and we had lost the people's respect. Of course the traders should never have been allowed to sell the stolen German and Italian stores. All enemy army stores should have been confiscated from the start.

Almost immediately after our arrival in Tripoli, ships began to come into the harbour, and our battalion, with others, supplied the dock labour. At first we made our own arrangements with the Navy and the engineers in charge of the docks and the unloading proceeded quickly and smoothly, but after a few days Area Command took over and the organisation deteriorated at once. We would get an order to supply eighty men to report at the docks at 6 A.M. The order would not come through until about midnight; this meant calling officers and N.C.O.s out of bed and laying on special breakfasts, which had to be cooked in darkness without breaking the black-out. Fuel was very scarce and we had not sufficient petrol to use our petrol cookers and normally used wood collected by fatigue-men. An open fire was out of the question during the hours of darkness, and so we had to use our precious petrol. The men had to wash and dress in the dark and have breakfast in the dark, standing around the cook-house. We had no buildings, and often it was raining hard. It was $2\frac{1}{2}$ miles to the docks, and this meant leaving the camp at about 5 A.M. and a 4 A M.

reveille! Our companies were depleted, and it was almost impossible to supply the numbers asked for, after allowing for battalion and divisional guards and all the other multitudinous tasks which were piling up on us. We would finally scrape every available man together, and, after giving them a semi-cold breakfast, march them down to the docks, where time and again no one was there to give instructions. The Navy were still asleep and very disgruntled if awakened, and often we would find a party from another battalion who had been detailed for the same job. The men would have to hang about until after 9 A.M. before any work started, and it can be imagined what they felt and said. Our adjutant tried to do something about it, and we used to take great pleasure in trying to get the staff officers concerned out of their beds to give us instructions. These difficulties are seldom heard of by the Higher Command, and I am quite sure that if they had become known very drastic action indeed would have been taken against those responsible.

Another source of great irritation was that after the first few days the Staff wallahs from Cairo moved into the Grand Hotel. By this time we were able to have hot baths there, and as it was the only place where such facilities were available, we took full advantage of it. The Staff wallahs promptly made an order that these facilities had to be withdrawn from all except those staying at the hotel. This was followed shortly by an order forbidding the hotel staff to serve dinner (brought in by ourselves) to any but residents. From this it was a short step to closing the bar to us, and within a week we found ourselves excluded altogether. Now the W.O.s and N.C.O.s and men all had proper clubs to go to, but we officers who had fought right through the campaign now found that the only place available to us was taken away by those who had lived in comfort and safety while we were fighting. We were naturally furious, and some of the younger bloods were for " beating up " the place and its residents. As a kind of sop to us, they opened up a second-rate little ice-cream shop where for exorbitant prices one could buy a minute glass of three types of sweet wine. All these types tasted exactly the same, the place was packed out, and there were no facilities for sitting down or writing, and often even this bar shut for lack of supplies. Some of us found another little hotel farther down the promenade, and we used to take eggs there and have them cooked as omelettes, but in less than a week this place also was taken over by a major of the Catering Corps, to be turned into a " rest home " for tired officers. It was useless to say that if anyone had a claim to that title it was ourselves. After the first week we did not bother to go into the town at all.

In spite of these irritations, life at Tripoli was very pleasant. My company had won a large Italian bell-tent, and we used to invite other officers in to supper and bridge and we had some very cheery parties. On arrival at Tripoli I had taken over command of the company, and I couldn't have had a happier and cheerier crowd of officers. All old hands, two of them had been wounded at Alamein and rejoined the day after we arrived at Tripoli; we got on famously, and after we got over the first disappointment of Tripoli we made the best of a bad job and enjoyed life to the full. There was very little training; for by the time one had found all the working parties required, there were no men left to train. The men were kept pretty busy, and certainly did not have the holiday and rest which had been promised to them, but as there was nothing to do anyway, nobody regretted that much.

Early in February we heard that a great personage was coming to inspect us. Speculation varied between the King, Winston Churchill, and Stalin! There was a great bustling about, exchanging of battle-dress and issue of new flashes, and rehearsals. These rehearsals bored and irritated the men, who, after a long night of working at the docks, intensely disliked the cleaning up and marching down to the promenade and the organised cheering of an empty car, representing the " high personage," but when Churchill finally arrived the men gave him a great reception, and the march-past with massed pipes and drums playing the regimental marches was most impressive. We got a half-day holiday after the parade was over. The time passed very quickly, and on 18th February we marched out of Tripoli on the first stage of our journey up to the front.

## CHAPTER XI.

### EARLY DAYS IN FRONT OF THE MARETH LINE.

THE first three days of the journey up the line was by route-march, and we covered a distance of over fifty miles. The men were in good spirits and not sorry to leave Tripoli. We all expected another break-through and a quick chase into Tunis, and speculation was rife whether Tunis would be a second Tripoli. The general attitude was summed up by one Jock, who said, " Anyway, it will be another damned foreign town with no proper pubs and nothing but restrictions, but the sooner we get there the sooner we'll be back in Glasgow."

The second stage of the journey was by troop-carrier. We crossed over the Tunisian border, and as we passed along the road we saw signs of the fighting which had been going on continuously while we were in Tripoli. The armoured division had had no rest like us, but following up the retreating enemy, had fought a skilful rearguard action right back to the Medenine positions in front of the Mareth Line, which they were now holding. Even after we arrived our front was very thinly held, not because we lacked the men but because we could not keep a large force supplied. Our supply lines were strained to their limit. The bulk of supplies were still coming over a thousand miles of indifferent roads, and what came by sea had to run the gauntlet of enemy submarines and aircraft. Dangerous bottle-necks had to be avoided in harbours partially destroyed and filled with sunken hulks. It was a miracle of skilful organisation that we were able to maintain any army at all so far from its base.

On the night of the 24th February we took over a sector of the widely dispersed front. Everything was very quiet ; the enemy were about two miles away, and they might have been a hundred for all the sign they showed that they were there. We took up a position to the north of the Medenine road, the main road to Mareth. The position was a series of platoon areas about a mile and a half in front of a low ridge of sand-hills. The ground was divided into sectors by wadis, which ran almost parallel with the front. In front of us was a wide, flat, and slightly rising plateau, and in the distance a range of fairly high hills with a few sugar-loaf hills which appeared at first to be part of the main range, but were in fact several miles in front. Rumours were passing that Rommel was about to launch a large counter-attack, taking advantage of our weakness on the ground. For a week we patrolled vigorously, and the rumours became fact. Rommel was going to attack. The American 2nd Corps had suffered a reverse at Kasserine, and apparently Rommel had switched the bulk of his armour to this sector to follow up their retreat. This probably saved us from an immediate attack, and appears to have been a tactical blunder on Rommel's part, for his attack would have had a far greater chance of success at that time than it was to have when he finally launched it. On these patrols we went far into enemy territory, dodging round minefields and always fishing for information. Wandering Arabs passed along the tracks going from the British side to the German, impartially exchanging information of the two sides' movements. It was an interesting week of waiting and a very active one.

On the night of the 3rd March, second-in-command of companies (my company commander had taken over the company again after we left Tripoli), with working parties, were pulled out and taken back to the line of sandy hills two miles behind platoon positions. I worked all the following day on these positions, and had only turned in at 3 A.M. the following morning when I was called up by the commanding officer and told to go out and bring in the company. The other companies had been pulled back the evening before, leaving only my company out. The plan was to deceive the enemy into thinking that we still held the original forward positions. He would then plan his time of attack accordingly, and rush in for the final attack just at dawn to find the birds had flown. The effect would be somewhat like a man charging at a supposedly barred door, only to find when he couldn't stop himself that the door was not shut. In the resultant bewilderment we hoped to give him all we had, for we had the positions well taped, and, if he did decide to continue the attack, he would have to do it in daylight against strong positions from which we had an ideal field of fire.

It was very dark when I set out with two of the Intelligence section to guide me, and my batman making the fourth. The Intelligence men were to guide me back to the old Battalion H.Q. *via* the wadi tracks. This was a long way round, but the C.O. thought that I would be more likely to get lost going straight across country. In actual fact I would have much preferred the latter course, for I had memorised various landmarks, and the wadi tracks were numerous and twisting and entailed doubling back on one's route more than once. The Intelligence men were none too sure of the way and nor was I. We wasted a precious hour finding the old Battalion H.Q., and then the most difficult part of the journey lay ahead. I had only been once back between the company position and Battalion H.Q., and that was by daylight. It was difficult enough then, for the ground was a series of folds, each identical to the next, and troops entrenched in such ground were invisible by day let alone during a pitch-black night. It was essential that I got the company out before dawn, for the attack was definitely expected that morning, and in fact the enemy was reported as being already on their way. I looked anxiously at my watch as I set off across the intervening ground in what I hoped was the direction of the company positions. A hundred yards' error on either side was sufficient to let me walk right past the position without knowing it, unless there was a very observant sentry. I dared not call out in case the enemy had scouts out in front of their advancing forces. At night one is always inclined to overestimate distances, but after twenty minutes' hard walking I was sure I ought to be level with the positions. I called gently, at the same time peering into the gloom; there was no reply. I carried on a little farther and tried again; there was still no reply. I began to feel panicky, for time was passing quickly. I started walking in ever-growing arcs, stopping to call from time to time. Everything was very still; the only sound was the faint rustling of the wind through the long desert grass. I was getting frantic with worry when at four o'clock, after trying to left and right and having gone half-way back to my starting-point, I still hadn't found them.

I had just decided to throw caution to the wind and shout at the top of my voice when I heard voices in the distance. Making my way towards them I suddenly saw a stone hut looming up in the shadows. I stopped abruptly; there was no hut on my company's sector. Where had I got to? A wild thought rushed through my mind that I had walked right into the enemy positions without realising how far I had gone. I had heard of people doing that; then I realised it was absolutely ridiculous; the enemy positions were at least three miles away. I frantically tried to recall the map in my mind, where had there been shown a stone hut? I couldn't recall one at all, except for a "keep" at least a mile and a half in front of our company position. Had I reached that? I crept up to the wall of the hut and listened, my batman lying back covering me. My relief was intense when I heard good Scots voices. Still utterly bewildered as to my whereabouts, but greatly relieved that I was at least still in our own lines, I went in and found a patrol of another regiment just about to set off back to their Battalion H.Q. They had been occupying the hut for much the same purpose as my company were lying out, and had received orders to pull out. My distance out was just right, but I was much too far to the left, right in another battalion area. I set off again, walking parallel to the front. It was already beginning to show signs of getting light, so I broke into a run. I was tired out, but felt I must get there; my batman stumbled along behind me cursing.

I arrived at the company position just as the first streaks of light were stretching across the sky. I was so breathless I could hardly speak, but gasped out, " You have to withdraw at once; the attack is expected this morning," and collapsed on the ground. One of the officers gave me a swig from his whisky flask which pulled me together. The company had been prepared for an immediate withdrawal, and were soon on the move. I explained what was happening. The company commander suggested my going back in the 15-cwt. truck and taking a different route from the company so as not to attract attention. I thankfully agreed. I was ready to risk any enemy shooting for the chance of a drive back. Sinking thankfully into the seat beside the driver, we set off back. There was no sign of the enemy. The attack had not come in as expected. I often wonder if I should have arrived in time if it had come in, and if not what would have happened.

We all got back safely and settled in our new positions. I was out on an early patrol that night, and reported on my return that I had heard sounds of vehicles moving. We stood-to at daybreak, and the expected attack came in.

# CHAPTER XII.

### ROMMEL ATTACKS.

It was just at daybreak on the 4th March that our outposts reported enemy troops advancing. A platoon of our company had been pushed out in front to give the enemy the impression that we were still holding the forward positions, and to ensure by firing on them that they opened out for the final attack in the area of our old positions, which were now closely covered by fire from artillery, machine-guns, and mortars. This platoon was now engaging the enemy, and we could hear the Bren guns rattling.

I had left Company H.Q. to take over a forward platoon which was dug in on a hill to the left of our main positions. We had been warned that the enemy would probably infiltrate through our thinly extended line, and were prepared in each platoon locality for a three-day siege. It was intended that the main battle should take place on the wide plain well behind our positions, where an ideal "killing ground" had been chosen. We had ammunition and food for three days dug in round the section posts, and in our deep trenches we felt quite confident that we could hold out and beat off any attempts to take our positions by assault. This kind of war was a novelty to us. Up to the present time we had always been the ones out in the open, being shot up as we advanced, and now we were comfortably settled in our deep holes with nothing to do but shoot at the advancing hordes of green and khaki-clad men. I made a last dash round the section posts, and as I reached my own hole, which as usual I was sharing with my batman, a burst of machine-gun fire swept over the crest of our hill. Owing to a rise in the ground in front of us, we could not see whether the battle plan had succeeded (I learnt afterwards that it couldn't have been more successful. The enemy fell right into the trap and rushed at our deserted forward positions, and on realising they were empty stood round bewildered ; the machine-guns opened up on them, and men fell like ninepins. They did, however, make a rapid recovery, and after pulling back behind a ridge re-formed and advanced again). During their advance the enemy had pushed their machine-gun teams forward, and these, having approached within three hundred yards of our new positions, had opened up to cover the advancing infantry. About half an hour after the first shots were fired the platoon which had been out in front returned without casualties and took up their prepared positions. They were followed almost immediately by the first wave of enemy infantry.

These were a mixed bag of Germans in the khaki uniform of the Afrika Korps and Italians in their dark-green tunics. They advanced by sections in close formation, and offered an admirable target. I took over a Bren gun myself, and, shouting to the others to hold their fire, waited until they were within four hundred yards ; then I gave the signal, and we let them have magazine after magazine. All along the front we could hear the Brens and rifles cracking. The enemy sections stopped, wavered, broke into a double, and pushed on, stopped again, and finally dived for shelter among some scattered olive trees. They must have suffered terrible casualties. We reloaded and waited ; there was a long pause ; over on our left in the direction of Medenine we could hear what we guessed was a tank battle in progress, the deep rumbling of the tanks and the sharp crack of the six-pounders. The guns would flare into a fury and then die down to an occasional shot. After about half an hour's complete lull on our sector we heard the rattling of machine-guns and the crackle of rifles from the company on our left. We could see only the crest of the hill they were occupying, but knew at once that another attack was going in.

There was still no sign of movement on our own front. Occasionally we spotted a single enemy soldier getting up and running doubled up from cover to cover. Our snipers kept continual watch, and winged quite a few of these. Then there was a roar overhead, and two planes screamed down, skimming the crest of the hill as they swooped up again; we could see the bombs falling, and immediately after there was a series of deafening explosions. The company on our right had caught the bombs right on its positions. I learnt after that they had had a few casualties, including killed. Shortly after, the enemy started to mortar our position. It was unpleasant but not very effective; for we were too well dug in to suffer from anything except a direct hit.

The day dragged on, and though there were several false alarms the expected attack did not materialise, and by 5.30 P.M. in the evening there was almost complete silence along the whole of our battalion front.

About 5.45 P.M. my company commander came across to me and said it had been decided that I should lead a counter-attack against the enemy and drive them out of the wadi which had been our original Battalion H.Q. and in which they were now collected. I was to have two tanks in support and was not to go beyond the wadi. I was to take one platoon, and the rest of the company would give me covering fire. There was no time to ask questions, for zero hour had been fixed for 6 P.M.; but it did seem to me a very light force with which to launch a counter-attack. I barely had time to give out orders before we had to start. We crawled out of our trenches and formed up just behind the crest of the ridge in front of our position. I hastily disposed my small force and lay down on my stomach watching the hands of my watch moving towards six o'clock. Two minutes to go and no sign of the two tanks! Another two minutes crept by and still no tanks. The men were getting nervy and so was I. Another half-minute ticked by. . . . I knew that if the tanks were even on their way up I should be bound to hear them.

It was no use waiting. I gave the signal and we jumped up and advanced. The moment we showed ourselves over the crest of the ridge we were greeted by a hail of machine-gun bullets, but, by nothing short of a miracle, we did not have a single casualty, and in a few paces we were again covered by a fold in the ground. About two hundred yards half-right on a slight rise in the ground was a .broken-down Arab hut. I knew it had been occupied during the afternoon by the enemy, and I detailed two men with hand-grenades to crawl up and blow them out. Meanwhile I continued to advance steadily. I heard the explosion of the grenades and saw one German doubling hard down the dip behind the hut. Now we were on the next crest, and on our left there was the sound of heavy machine-gun firing. A few bullets were whistling past us, and one embedded itself in the ground just in front of me. One man was shot through the leg; then I saw in the distance on my left a crowd of khaki figures making towards our left-hand company's positions. It flashed through my mind that the enemy had chosen the same time as we to launch an attack. There was no sign of any enemy on my immediate front and those on my left offered an ideal target. I decided that this was an occasion when it was permissible to be diverted from one's main objective. I halted and took cover against a broken stone wall which bordered a cultivated patch, and, wheeling my left-hand section round, pointed out the target and gave the order to open fire. For once I had field-glasses with me and could follow the course of the bullets (every one in ten was tracer). I looked again at the khaki figures and then realised to my horror that they were our own troops. I shouted cease fire and stared again. Yes, they were certainly our own men. I couldn't think what they were doing, but decided that they must have launched a local attack and were now on their way back. We had only fired one burst, and from the course of the tracers I reckoned that this burst had gone over their heads, so I hoped we had not inflicted any casualties. We advanced again, and then ran into heavy mortar fire. My sergeant was hit, and I decided to take cover in a shallow wadi. I was now only about fifty yards from the wadi that was my objective.

British or Commonwealth troops in action during the fighting at El Alamein in 1942. (HMP)

British or Commonwealth troops watch as fires burn over Tobruk prior to the fighting of the Second Battle of El Alamein. (HMP)

General Erwin Rommel and General Fritz Bayerlein (both standing) survey Tobruk following its fall on 21 June 1942. Following Tobruk's capture, Churchill declared: "This was one of the heaviest blows I can recall during the war. Not only were its military effects grievous, but it had affected the reputation of the British armies." (Bundesarchiv, Bild 101I-785-0299-22A/Moosmüller/CC-BY-SA)

British vehicles, in the background, pass the shattered remains of an Italian field gun position. (HMP)

Rommel and Bayerlain pictured in Tobruk itself. Note the Allied PoWs on the left of the shot. Some 35,000 Allied troops were captured by the Germans, including the bulk of the the 2nd South African Infantry Division. (Bundesarchiv, Bild 101I-785-0299-07A/Moosmüller/CC-BY-SA)

A Stuart tank travelling at speed near Mount Imeimat in the Western Desert on 26 August 1942, during the lead-up to the Second Battle of El Alamein later that year. (HMP)

An unofficial war artist, Lance Bombardier Aston Fuller was serving as a member of the Royal Artillery with the 51st Highland Division in North Africa. This example of his artwork shows a soldier "repairing the line of communication" at a Forward Observation Post during the Battle of El Alamein in October 1942. Aston's original caption states: "The last ridge held by the Germans was taken. The Scots named it 'The Nairn'. It had to be held – and it was. The 'eyes of the guns' were able to over-look the enemy positions. Signallers worked under heavy fire to try and keep the line of communications open – exposure meant instant death!" (Courtesy of Gwyneth Wilkinson; custodian of the original artwork)

British tanks move up to the battle to engage the German armour after the infantry had cleared gaps in the enemy minefield at El Alamein, 24 October 1942. (HMP)

A British Crusader tank passes a burning German Pzkw Mk.IV tank during the fighting in North Africa. (HMP)

A mobile anti-tank unit of the Eighth Army in action somewhere in the desert in North Africa in 1942. (HMP)

A British patrol is on the lookout for enemy movements over a valley in the Western Desert, 1942. (HMP)

"Australians storm a strongpoint". Taken by Army photographer Sergeant Len Chetwyn, this classic photograph of the Desert War, taken in early November 1942, was actually a fake, staged at rear headquarters using Australian troops. Nevertheless, it became one of the Second World War's most famous images. (HMP)

Wearing his famous beret, Lieutenant General B.L. Montgomery, General Officer Commanding Eighth Army, watches the beginning of the German retreat from El Alamein from the turret of his Grant Tank, 5 November 1942. (HMP)

Another drawing by Signaller Aston Fuller, this time entitled "A Forward Patrol Post, Mareth Line Front, March 1943". Aston's original caption states: "The day draws to a close. The fast receding light sees the Forward Patrol of the gun position move out. An officer leads as his NCO and men disappear over the ridge. Darkness now falls. Stars begin to twinkle in the sky – there is no moon. The air is crisp and cold, so men are wrapped in mufflers and greatcoats with gloves over mittens." (Courtesy of Gwyneth Wilkinson; custodian of the original artwork)

The end of the fighting in North Africa. This picture, taken from an Army observation aircraft, shows some of the hundreds of thousands of Axis prisoners of war captured in May 1943. (HMP)

Major Hugh Peter de Lancy Samwell MC is buried in grave XI. A. 11. in Hotton War Cemetery, Belgium. The village of Hotton was the western limit of the German counter offensive in the Ardennes in January 1945. The majority of the burials in Hotton War Cemetery date from that time. (Courtesy of the Commonwealth War Graves Commission)

The mortaring continued, but changed from heavy explosives to smoke. I peered over the edge and saw the ground rising in a gentle slope from the other side of our objective, and over this ground the enemy were pouring back in confusion. The machine-gunning had stopped, so we jumped up and rushed forward. We ran as hard as we could, stopping from time to time to fire at the retreating enemy. The smoke from the smoke-bombs was pouring across our front and we could only get occasional glimpses of our target through it.

On reaching the wadi I realised it was hopeless to try and catch them up; they had at least a four hundred yards' start. I let the men fire into the thick smoke and hoped that a few bullets would find a billet. The wadi itself was completely deserted except for the usual junk of battle. I re-formed my platoon and was just considering my next move when an officer from the right-hand company came up with a body of men. I asked him what he was doing; he told me that he had also had orders to attack at 6 P.M. and that he was to coincide his attack with mine. He had started immediately he saw me starting, and had been on my right throughout the advance. I was surprised that I had not been told of this when given my orders. We consulted each other, and decided that as it was fast getting dark there was nothing more to be done and we should make our way back to our companies independently. At that moment the two tanks arrived. I told them rather shortly that they were too late, but suggested that they patrol the length of the wadi in case any of the enemy were still lurking in it. The other officer went with them in order to guide them back afterwards, and I made my way back to Company H.Q. My total casualties were a sergeant and two men wounded.

On reporting back I was received with great relief. They had heard all the firing of our Brens and had feared the worst. I gave an account of what had happened, stressing that the enemy had made no attempt to stop and fight. I was told then that the counter-attack had been launched by one platoon from each company, that the synchronisation had been bad, and that the extreme left company had started too soon, had met considerable opposition, and for lack of support had had to pull out. It was this company that I had fired on. They must have started well before six o'clock; for it was not five minutes past six when I had first noticed them on their way back. The two tanks eventually came back, but one of them had a track blown off by blundering into our own minefield.

Thus ended Rommel's much-boosted attack, for all along the line he had been beaten off, and only at Medenine itself had his tanks succeeded in infiltrating a little way, to meet with terrible punishment from our tanks. From the stores left behind, we won hundreds of packets of American cigarettes and chocolate which the Germans had recently taken from the Americans at Kasserine. These prizes were very welcome; for we had been reduced to cutting a " V " cigarette into three and having a third of a cigarette in the morning, another third in the afternoon, and the last third after supper. The chocolate was an almost unheard-of luxury.

## CHAPTER XIII.

#### PATROLS AND KEEPS.

It was an hour later. I had only just finished supper when my company commander told me that I was to take a patrol out that night to find out what the enemy were doing, and bring in any wounded or lost men whom they might have left behind. It was rather a shock to learn that I had to go out again so soon after the evening's affair, and I asked and was granted permission to take out fresh men. In fact I had no trouble in getting volunteers. The news of the captured American cigarettes had got around, and was quite enough incentive for men who had been reduced to smoking cactus leaves for almost a week. It was the only time throughout the campaign that we were really short of cigarettes. The supply question was so serious that the High Command had rightly decided that all luxuries would have to be held up until sufficient food and ammunition had been brought up to safeguard our rather precarious positions at the end of a supply line so extended as to be almost snapping. The acute shortage had produced quite a few comic incidents. Shortly before the attack we had had a visit from a high commander and some of his staff. These officers had stood round in a group talking to our commanding officer about the impending attack. A crowd of men had quickly gathered round them, and somebody remarked on the very unusual display of curiosity shown by these men, for brass-hats were usually the sign for every man to disappear into the nearest hole. Our own officers were puzzled too, until they saw the men making a quick dive to retrieve the fag-ends thrown away by many of the Staff officers who were smoking. In actual fact the shortage only affected the forward companies. In the higher formations it is always possible to carry reserves of Naafi stores in the many trucks attached to

H.Q.s, and our own quartermaster had quite a large reserve. Thus Battalion H.Q. and H.Q. company were kept reasonably well supplied, but the supplies did not extend up to the forward companies. This is always a cause of grievance between the " fighting " soldiers and H.Q. personnel.

I started out about 11 P.M. that night; there was a gentle rain falling and we were wet through. It was a very dark night, and at first I could not find even the wadi, until I discovered that I had happened to come on it at a spot where the banks sloped gently down into it and had walked right across it without realising. We walked along the whole length of it, as far as the boundaries of our battalion front, without seeing or hearing anything. There were a few rifles lying about and a carrier that we had had to abandon when we pulled out the day before. One of the men reported that he thought he had stepped on a partly buried body, but when we turned back we could not find the place. After an hour I gave it up and pushed out towards the enemy lines. There were sounds of great transport activity, and from time to time Very lights shot up into the night. We went right up to their minefields, and after lying up listening for a while, I decided to return. I got back about 3.30 A.M. and made a negative report. My company commander was frankly unbelieving; my negative report just did not tally with the account I had given of my counter-attack. Then I had stated that we had fired on the retreating enemy, and, in spite of the smoke and growing dusk, were certain that we had inflicted casualties. Now we were asking him to believe that we could not find a single wounded man or even a corpse. I appreciated his difficulty in believing me; I could scarcely believe it myself, but facts were facts.

The company commander decided to send out another officer with a fresh patrol. I was annoyed at this, for it showed me too obviously that he thought I had not done my job; but there was nothing I could do about it, and I went back to my trench and tried to sleep. I was wet through, and it was now raining heavily and the bottom of my trench was already six inches deep in water. I lowered myself gingerly into the muddy bottom and felt the water seeping through my garments. Eventually I did doze off, but only for half an hour, when I was awakened for stand-to. The sun came up strongly that morning and I was soon dry again. The second patrol had returned just before stand-to, also with a negative report. I was relieved at this; for if they had managed to find anything of interest it certainly would have looked as if I had not done my job.

The C.O. came up after breakfast and suggested that I should take a small patrol out again and have a search in daylight. I was not keen, for I was very tired and stiff; however, I set off half an hour later. When I arrived at the wadi I found heaps of discarded kit left in the dug-outs which had been dug into the walls of the wadi. In one of these I found a corpse, and farther along another three corpses which had been hastily buried and whose limbs were still protruding from the sand. I took regimental badges and papers off these bodies and was about to return when I heard my name called.

Climbing out of the wadi I found the assistant carrier officer with two German prisoners. I asked him where he had found them, and he replied that they were asleep in a dug-out in the wadi. I examined them, and saw that they were mere boys. They readily gave me all the particulars I asked. One told me that he was only sixteen years old and had been out in Africa less than three weeks. He had been training at a submarine school near Hamburg when he was suddenly ordered to join a draft of soldiers who were leaving for the front. He had had no training as a soldier apart from the training given in the Hitler Youth Movement, and had not been allowed even to say good-bye to his parents. He had not known which front he was going to, and he and his companions had been very relieved when they discovered that it was not Russia. He thought it was a great mistake that the British and Germans were fighting each other; he knew many English people in Hamburg and liked them. Hamburg had been badly bombed, and work at the docks was almost at a stand-still. He thought the British did not understand that the Germans were only fighting to defend Europe from the Bolshevists, and the British of all people should be fighting with the Germans for such a purpose. " Would he have a chance to explain this to the British authorities ? " He was obviously genuine in his beliefs, and was, I think, a typical example of one of Hitler's dupes. He was quite glad to be a prisoner, and said he knew the British would treat him well, and when they discovered their mistake, which he hoped would not be too late, he would readily volunteer to fight with them in the crusade against Bolshevism.

In the following weeks we were to capture many boys like this, who had clearly been taught the line they were to take if captured. The Bolshevist menace and Britain's ghastly mistake in fighting on the wrong side came out like a gramophone record, and scarcely varied in words and never in theme. The other boy was rather surly, and did not approve of his companion's friendliness. I asked them what they had been doing when they were captured, and they replied that they had gone to sleep, and when they woke up they had found themselves all alone, and then the carrier officer had come and they had given themselves up. It sounded rather a tall story to me, for I could not imagine them sleeping through all the previous evening's battle even if their officers had allowed them. There was little doubt that they were deserters. One of my men asked me to ask them what Tunis was like. They replied that it was a dull place with nothing to do and nothing worth buying, and that the people were unfriendly to them. They had only been there three days before moving up to the front.

A further search revealed a large amount of stores and weapons which somehow we had missed the previous night, but I returned still puzzled about what had happened to the many wounded and killed there must have been along the battalion front as a result of the whole day's fighting. It is still a mystery.

That afternoon, while I was trying to get a little sleep, I had another visit from the C.O. This time he wanted me to take a platoon out and establish a keep about $3\frac{1}{2}$ miles in front of our positions. From there I could patrol and generally keep an eye on the enemy's movements.

I set out that night with thirteen specially chosen men and an artillery observation officer with a wireless truck. An Arab hut lay 200 yards ahead on the top of a small hill. It was an ideal place from which to observe the enemy's movements, but, on the other hand, it was a very prominent feature and would certainly be under observation, and impossible for anyone to approach during daylight without being seen by the enemy.

I posted two men in the building, and then took a small patrol forward to find out what the enemy were doing. Everything was very quiet, and we returned within an hour to our base. This keep was situated in a deep wadi which wound its way in continuous coils. The general direction was from north to south—*i.e.*, from our lines to the enemy's—but in my section there was a particularly wide coil which almost completed a circle. It was possible to lie hidden in here for days and move about quite freely; for unless enemy patrols chanced upon it by luck they could walk past it within fifty yards without realising it was there at all. About two hundred yards to the right was a well-cultivated olive grove, and shortly after dawn we heard the sound of a motor starting up from that direction. We went out to investigate, and on arriving at the grove saw the fresh tracks of a vehicle already marked in the sand which was still wet from the morning dew. We had the company of the enemy within two hundred yards of us without knowing it. I trusted that they had been equally ignorant of our presence. There was little we could do during the day except keep watch. I spent an hour memorising every feature, and reconnoitring a route of withdrawal in case we had to pull out in a hurry, and then I had a much-needed sleep.

In the afternoon I was awakened by the sound of shells exploding near us, and found to my amazement that they were coming from our own guns. I did not want to use the wireless if I could avoid it; for we were too near the enemy, and it would draw their attention to our presence, but when a shell landed within twenty yards of us I felt that this was too much of a good thing and I asked the gunner officer to get on to his own battery. He did so, and spoke with some feeling. The shooting went on, however, for another ten minutes, fortunately without inflicting any casualties on our party, though that was not the gunners' fault. We learnt afterwards that a frantic message was sent round to stop the firing, and eventually it was traced to a unit who, blissfully ignorant of our presence, had chosen our olive grove for sighting tests. Either the shooting or our wireless had attracted the enemy's attention, for an hour later, just before dusk, an enemy patrol twelve strong came out to investigate.

I had a standing patrol out at the time and the N.C.O. in charge was searching the front with his field-glasses when a bullet spat into the ground beside him. He went to ground and fired in the direction from which the bullet had come. It must have been a lucky shot; for a man broke from cover and disappeared quickly into the shrubs adjoining the olive grove. I never found out whether this lone sniper had any connection with the patrol or not; the latter was winding its way towards the olive grove, but was still about four hundred yards away. I decided to try and surround it in the olive grove. We got into position and watched it advancing. The enemy were making no attempt to advance in formation, but were trailing along one behind the other in a careless fashion. They disappeared from our view as they approached the grove, and I lost my chance to deal with them. I had forgotten about the comparatively deep dip on the far side. We heard them moving about in the grove and tried to stalk them, but it was growing dark, and search as we did we couldn't find them. It was clear that they were aware of our presence, for we heard them moving quickly away as we approached. This game went on for about half an hour, and then, fearing that I might be surprised in the rear if they had managed to get word back, I called off the hunt and returned to the wadi. Meanwhile the gunner officer had got word back to the battalion through his own battery, my direct wireless connection having failed to get through.

The Germans, who had got on to our wave-length, were deliberately damping our signals, and it was only with the greatest difficulty that I could hear the orders issued from the battalion. Apparently they wanted me to pull out at once, but I wasn't quite sure, and I had been given authority to use my own discretion in everything; therefore I decided to remain and try to find out more about the enemy's intentions. I sent out a listening patrol a hundred yards ahead, and when it was dark enough pulled in the observation post. We could still hear the patrol moving about in the olive grove, and I decided, after consultation with the gunner officer, to try and beat them out by getting our battery to shoot up the area of the olive grove. This was risky, for we ourselves were only two hundred yards at the most from the grove; but I could not afford to allow the enemy to remain there during the night, particularly as they were almost astride of our line of withdrawal. The gunner officer directed the firing, and the first shell landed about two hundred yards to our right. All secrecy had now gone; for his voice, as he spoke into the microphone, echoed out in the still evening air. The bracketing was most successful, and then they gave the grove a good plastering. We had one or two narrow shaves, but no one was hurt. We lay waiting for our quarry to break cover, but they made no move. After the shelling had finished we made another search of the grove; it was now quite dark, but the birds had flown. They must have worked round and out the other side, the grove being too big for me to cover with the small force I had.

All night we patrolled, and at 3 A.M. a patrol returned to report signs of enemy movement on a fairly large scale. It was clear they were going to stage a dawn attack on us. Just at that moment a message came through from the battalion ordering us to return at once. I had just decided that there was no point in remaining longer, for our positions had been taped by the enemy, so we filtered out noiselessly. I learnt afterwards that the position was attacked in strength at dawn, the knowledge coming to me by a strange coincidence, through a wounded German officer who was in the same casualty clearing station as I, and who had led the attack. He was wounded and captured a day later on another sector.

Our return journey was uneventful until the very last lap. I was rather anxious about the noise the wireless truck made and expected the enemy to open up on us every moment, but not a shot was fired. I parted with the gunner officer and his truck when about a mile or less from our own lines and then walked into disaster in the shape of a mine. I was told afterwards that it was actually I who stood on it; whether that be true or not I do not know, but just as our own wire came in sight and I had turned round to the men following me and said, " Well, we are safely back," we were thrown to the ground by a loud explosion. I was completely stunned at first, and then realised that I was wounded. Eight out of the fourteen of my party were casualties. It was maddening to have come through all the dangers of the past two days only to be blown up at the home stretch. My wounds were not serious, though I had to be helped in, both legs being splattered with bits of shrapnel. I was quickly taken back to the R.A.P., where the doctor dressed the larger wounds. I was able to make a full report to the commanding officer and Intelligence officer before being taken back to the advanced dressing station. On the way back the road was shelled and I had rather a fright, but we got through safely and soon I was on the way back to Tripoli, *via* the casualty clearing station.

## CHAPTER XIV.

#### HOSPITAL IN TRIPOLI.

I SPENT two nights at the casualty clearing station, and it was on the second night that the German officer was brought in who had led the patrol against me in the keep. He was quite a friendly chap, and as he was in the next bed to mine we started talking. I do not think the majority of inmates of the ward quite approved of this " fraternising with the enemy," but apart from a genuine interest in the other side of the picture, which in this case was particularly interesting to me, I had found from experience that the best way to get information of value out of the enemy was to engage him in ordinary conversation, and my knowledge of German, bad though it was, had always proved a great advantage in this.

The policy towards prisoners varied a great deal from unit to unit. The older veterans of the Eighth Army were generally inclined to treat them in a reasonably friendly manner without becoming too familiar, while newer units and non-fighting units were generally inclined to be stricter.

On the whole the fighting in the desert had been fairly clean, and the Red Cross had been respected by both sides. Sometimes there developed a spirit almost of comradeship between opposing sides. This was mainly because each side realised the other was suffering the same hardships, and so often the desert was more of an enemy than the official enemy. Recently, too, a very good impression had been given to our men by the good conditions in which our wounded were found in Tripoli Hospital. This was due entirely to the German medical staff. The treatment of our wounded by the Italians was at all times disgraceful. This was partly by intention, and partly because of their disgustingly primitive medical arrangements and their apparent complete ignorance of the need for cleanliness and normal sanitation.

Actual battles, however, were bitterly fought to the finish, neither side giving or expecting any favours. The official attitude was sometimes unnecessarily anxious about these signs of comradeship, and orders were issued from time to time discouraging any form of fraternising with prisoners. The atmosphere was to change completely when we got to Sicily, and met a different type of German altogether. There, after the first bitter experience of treating the battle like a hard-fought football match, we gave no quarter and got none.

I do not wish to give the impression that desert fighting was in any way half-hearted; it was ferocious and bitter, as the casualties well illustrated, but the tendency was to preserve the decencies, particularly with regard to wounded.

I discussed in detail with the German officer the conditions prevailing during that last night in the keep. He told me they had been suspicious from the first night that we had a force of some kind in the vicinity of the olive grove, and in the morning two ambulances had come in and reported hearing our voices; then in the afternoon they had recorded our shelling of the area, and this had puzzled them considerably. The only explanation they could think of was that their own troops were there and had been discovered by one of our patrols, which, being too weak to deal with them, had reported the location to the artillery. There had been considerable confusion after the failure of Rommel's attack, and whole platoons had got lost. They had also had trouble with conscripted Polish and Slovak elements, some of whom had taken the opportunity to desert. It was decided to send out a patrol at last light to investigate, and he had been chosen. Even when he had finally found us he was not able to judge how large the force was, and had finally decided to return to his H.Q. and suggest a full-scale attack. He had mistaken our wireless truck for a tank, and it was decided to attack on a two-company scale. The attack had gone in at 5.30 A.M. (two hours after we had left), and of course had drawn a blank. The same morning he was transferred to the sector south of Medenine, and had been captured, slightly wounded, on a patrol the same night.

Apart from the natural interest this had for me, I considered it of some value to our Intelligence and made a written report, which I sent back to the unit. A young gunner officer had been listening to our lengthy conversation with growing disapproval, and at last could not contain himself any longer. " I wish you would shut up," he burst out ; " it is a damned disgrace being so pally with a filthy Boche." I answered rather sharply, for I could see he had not followed the conversation, " If you have any complaint to make you know to whom to make it ; otherwise I suggest you don't interfere in matters you don't understand." He looked sheepish but sullen, and I realised on looking round that he had the sympathy of most of the ward. We often accuse the Germans of lack of imagination, but there is nothing to beat the stupidity of a certain type of Englishman who allows his whole life and actions to be governed by that stupid sentence, " It's not done." I was angry too, because I feared the German would understand, and I was anxious to carry on the conversation later and lead it into more general matters concerning the war, when I hoped that I might pick up some really valuable information. Just then an elderly Scots major, who was rather more seriously wounded than the rest of us, remarked, " Did you get any useful dope out of him ? " and grinned in a sympathetic manner. I returned the grin gratefully and nodded, and then seeing that the German had dozed off, replied, " Yes, and I would have got a lot more if that young idiot had more sense." Two hours later I was carried back into an ambulance for the last stage of my journey to Tripoli.

On arriving at Tripoli I was taken to the modern military hospital, built on high ground overlooking the town. It had only been completed in 1939 and was a very up-to-date establishment. The wards were large and airy, with specially designed sun windows and rolling shutters to keep out the glare. It had been run by a staff of nuns, who were still working there under the supervision of the R.A.M.C. They were nice little things, and I am afraid we teased them unceasingly when they came round making our beds and attending to our wants.

The Germans had put the fear of death in them before leaving by telling them that the British were half animal and would assuredly murder or rape them. They had been found locked in their chapel in the hospital trembling with fright, and still even after a month could not quite get over their fear of us. The one who attended to me spoke French, and each time she came I pretended to grab her, and she jumped back squealing with half-pretended, half-genuine fright. She said she could not understand how such friendly and innocent-looking boys could want to kill her poor, gentle Italian boys. We told her that she had got the story the wrong way round, and that it was her poor, gentle Italian boys who tried to kill us. She shook her head vehemently and cried over and over again, " I do not believe it." We told her that they tied time-bombs on to our wounded and tortured them, and that we had to run to the Germans for help, and she got very indignant and stamped her foot, saying, " You make fun of me all the time ; you make fun of me. It is not true ; my boys could not hurt a fly."

Sometimes she used to sit on the end of the bed, and her eyes would get big and serious, and she would shake her head sadly and say, " You men, why must you always fight and kill each other ; is there not really enough pain and misery in this world without you adding to it ? " And then she would pull out a rosary or picture of the Virgin Mary and slip it into my hand and tell me almost fiercely to pray for forgiveness. She asked me once if I had killed anyone, and when I replied, " Yes, many," she shrank back in horror and started crying, and I hastily said, " I was only teasing you ; I always shoot over their heads." She looked so relieved and happy that I felt my lie had been justified, and after that I'm afraid she spoilt me flagrantly, bringing me little extras at meal-times when the nursing sister wasn't looking. I felt rather a fraud, but had not the heart to disillusion her.

While I was in hospital we had many air raids, and some of the bombs dropped dangerously near. The shutters rattled and vibrated from the noise of the guns and bombs, and we felt very helpless lying in bed wondering if the next one was going to blow us to bits. One night they hit an ammunition ship in the harbour, and the explosions continued throughout the night. We could see the red glow of the fires showing through the black-out shutters.

After I had been in hospital ten days and was just able to hobble about a little with the aid of sticks, news came through that the hospital was to be cleared of all but the most serious cases to make room for large numbers of new casualties. We all knew what that meant: the attack on the Mareth Line was due. Those of us who were to be moved were either being sent back to the base hospitals in Egypt or, if fit enough, to the transit camp at Tripoli, where we could convalesce. I was a borderline case, and the surgeon gave me my choice. I did not feel I was bad enough to be evacuated right back to Egypt, and I shuddered at the thought of hitch-hiking my way back from Alexandria to Mareth or perhaps beyond. Although I had no particular desire to be in the next battle, I was anxious to be in at the kill, and I reckoned that if I took a week's convalescence at the transit camp I would rejoin the battalion in time for the final advance on Tunis. Another officer from my battalion left the hospital with me, and we got a truck to take us to the transit camp. This camp lay about a mile and a half out of the town, and as it was on the main road there was plenty of transport available to take us in and out. I was curious to know how much progress there had been in waking up the town since we had left it a month before, and the other officer and I went in that afternoon.

There was quite a good E.N.S.A. show on at the theatre and a cinema show at the Men's Club. We went to the theatre and afterwards to the Grand Hotel. It was possible, we had heard, to get afternoon tea there. We found the lounge packed with staff officers, and when we finally attracted the waiter's attention we learnt that we could get a small cup of coffee but nothing to eat. We ordered the coffee, and when it arrived, found it consisted of three mouthfuls of lukewarm water slightly flavoured with coffee essence. The bar was closed to all except residents, we were informed, and in the hall we saw a large notice stating, " Open to Residents only." We inquired if there was an officers' club, and were told there was not. We asked about the hotel which had been taken over for " tired officers," and were informed that this was now used as an overflow for the staff officers billeted in the town. There was the transit camp, of course, the clerk told us, and the " ice-cream shop " in the town. He suggested that we should make friends with a warrant officer and get an invitation to their club. So Tripoli had not changed! Combatant officers, wounded or otherwise, were not wanted there. We made our way back to the transit camp and drank down a mug of local " vino " in the bar. This " vino " was rationed to two per night, but one was sufficient to turn most stomachs.

We stayed here for five days. Nobody bothered about us, and if we had cared we could have stayed on indefinitely. There was one young artillery officer who had arrived with a draft from home in December last and had been there, he proudly told us, for three months. He said he had no intentions of going on unless he was told to. Fortunately most of the officers there were responsible and conscientious and only stayed as long as it was necessary to organise transport. This officer spent his time painting pictures from ' Men Only ' and other magazines, round the walls of the Mess, and I must admit that they were very good pictures. While we were at this transit camp we heard Churchill's broadcast, in which he announced the attack on the Mareth Line and in which he gave the first plans for the creation of a new and better Britain after the war. We went into Tripoli once or twice to the cinema. This was a very primitive affair showing very ancient films which came out a dirty sandy colour. The reproduction was so bad that it was almost impossible to make out what was being said. It was an attempt at entertainment, but a very poor one for a town which was now an important base and which had been in our hands for nearly two months. On the sixth day we got hold of a truck and, with two other officers, started back " up the line."

## CHAPTER XV.

### UP THE LINE AGAIN.

It was a fairly uneventful journey up the line again. The road was crammed with vehicles of all descriptions, and sometimes, for hours at a time, we had to crawl along behind a huge tank-carrier. We stopped the first night in a railway station at Zuara. The station yard had been turned into a R.A.S.C. depot and trucks were continually coming and going. The engineers were busy repairing the line and for miles along it African labour squads, under South African officers, were levelling the permanent way and relaying the lines, which had been torn up by the enemy during his retreat. Outside the station were the remains of a modern Diesel-engined carriage, with its highly polished chromium fittings and interior decorations contrasting with the battered outside plating. It had been blown up on the point system leading into the station. The town itself was an attractive mixture of modern Italian buildings and ancient Arab mosques. It was almost untouched by the war, which had raced past it before it properly realised what was going on. The British Administration had been set up in the town offices, and by a coincidence the officer in charge was an old member of our battalion who had left us after Alamein. At the entrance to his H.Q. he had a couple of hefty Arab sentries on duty dressed in elaborate coloured uniforms. We talked to him in the village square, and he invited us to lunch the following day, but we decided to push on and rejoin the battalion as soon as possible.

The next day we moved off early. It was grand to be independent of convoys and be able to start and stop in one's own time. We drove all day, stopping only for short spells to " brew up." We had brought three days' rations with us in case we could not find any transit camps. Rather disquieting news was coming back from the front by "R.A.S.C. telegraph," as we called the rumours passed down by the supply truck-drivers. The attack had failed and we were pulling back. First one division and then another were alleged to have had serious casualties. We passed convoys of ambulances, it is true, but not in such great numbers as to confirm these rumours. At Ben Gardane we stopped for the night at a transit camp. Even here we could get no authentic news. Everyone agreed that there had been a big action and that it had not succeeded in getting us through the Mareth Line; but after that, stories varied so much as to be quite unreliable.

While at Ben Gardane we visited the N.A.A.F.I., which had moved up there; we hoped to be able to buy a few cigarettes to take back to our companies, but the officer in charge refused to sell us even a packet for our own use. Whether he was within his rights or not I do not know, but it was all the more irritating after being refused to see members of the transit camp staff strolling across and buying as much as they wished. He was an aggressively rude youth whose authority had gone completely to his head. Although only a subaltern at that time (when I next saw him a week later he was a major), he was so used to being treated with deference by quite senior officers anxious to squeeze a few extras out of him for the Naafi-starved boys in the line, that he had learnt to treat all and sundry in the most offensive manner. We returned to the camp and I got an orderly to go over and buy me two hundred cigarettes, which he did without any trouble. The next day we started on the last stage of our journey, arriving about noon at a forward transit camp just beyond Medenine. There we learnt that the front had moved forward about three miles but that the frontal attack on the Mareth Line had failed, mainly because it had not been possible to get the anti-tank guns over an anti-tank ditch in time to support the infantry. The latter, left almost unsupported, had had a terrible time, and eventually had to be withdrawn. Our own division had not been concerned in this attack. Our

Divisional H.Q. was only a few miles away, and we decided to push on and rejoin our units that day. After a lot of searching we eventually found our " B " echelon, which was brigaded, and we stopped the night there as the guests of the quartermaster and transport officer.

The following morning we went to Battalion H.Q. and reported back. The battalion was in the line, but the enemy positions were out of small-arms range. There was a little shelling from both sides, but on the whole everything was very quiet. The commanding officer was surprised to see me back so soon, but when he saw how badly I was limping he sent me to the doctor, who promptly ordered me back to " B " echelon for at least ten days. Most of the shrapnel had been left in my legs and one piece was lodged behind my left knee, making it very stiff and painful to move, while a piece in the muscle of the right leg had caused my foot to go quite dead. I was not sorry to be left out of battle, for I was not feeling fit for any long marches.

The following night the Army mobile cinema came up to " B " echelon. We all sat in a wadi and the screen was erected with its back to the enemy, and there in the open we watched a two-hour performance. Both the film and the actual screening was far better than anything we had seen in Tripoli. The film, whose name I cannot remember, was the usual American one of night-life in New York; and, sitting there in the sand with the guns booming and flashing, it seemed almost uncanny to watch fashionably dressed men and women sitting down to luxurious meals in expensive night-clubs. We had a Donald Duck cartoon as well, and altogether it was a thoroughly good performance.

The next day the battalion advanced unopposed through the Mareth Line which had held us up for over a month. Monty had sent the New Zealanders round on his famous left hook, and the enemy, fearful of being surrounded, had fallen back to the Wadi Akarit by the town of Gabes.

I followed up the battalion with " B " echelon, passing through the area where the bitter hand-to-hand fighting had taken place a week before, when our attack had failed for lack of tank and anti-tank gun support. Burial parties and salvage squads were already at work, and Arab looters were wandering over the battlefields grabbing anything of value in spite of the attempts of our salvage troops to drive them off with rifle-fire. These Arabs often blew themselves up by standing on mines or climbing over booby-trapped barbed wire or picking up red devils (Italian hand-grenades). No sympathy was lost on these vile vultures, who descended on every battlefield immediately the action was over.

## CHAPTER XVI.

### LEFT OUT OF BATTLE.

The battalion moved up to an area about four miles east of the strong positions the enemy had taken up covering the " Gabes Gap." Everyone knew that a big battle was impending.

At the end of my first week at " B " echelon I went up to see the doctor again. The signal officer had been captured the previous day while leading the advance party up to the positions we were going to occupy; he had unfortunately overrun the positions and driven right into the enemy lines, where he had unsuccessfully attempted to fight his way out. As an old signal officer, the commanding officer wanted me to take over for the battle until he had the chance to look round for another. The doctor, however, said I was not fit and would not let me rejoin the battalion, so I made my way back to " B " echelon. There was a young officer among the L.O.B.s (left out of battle) who felt particularly aggrieved that he was always left out of the " party." That evening he received orders to report up the following morning to take over signals. Having poured out his grievances to me previously, he now came up to me beaming all over to tell me he was getting his chance. I was pleased for his sake; for he had been getting rather an inferiority complex about his position, and I knew that although he was by no means brilliant he had plenty of guts. He asked me to celebrate with him that night, and I stayed talking and drinking with him (he had " won " a bottle of whisky) until the early hours of the morning.

The next morning I went to Battalion H.Q. with him. He was as excited as a schoolboy, and had already planned how he was going to organise his new platoon. When he spoke about his " communication system " that he was going to try out during the battle, I had not the heart to discourage him by telling him that battles usually develop into a chaotic muddle, where preconceived " systems " rarely avail, and where " improvisation " is the order of the day. I went round the companies booking orders for the N.A.A.F.I., for I had decided that if I couldn't fight I could at least make myself useful by taking a truck back to Ben Gardane to collect N.A.A.F.I. stores.

I saw the young officer on my return to Battalion H.Q. busy checking his signal stores, and I wished him good luck. He grinned back cheerfully. He was killed early the next morning by an almost direct hit from a shell in his Signal H.Q.

That night I lay awake listening to the booming of the guns and the faint rattle of machine-guns. The battalion had moved up after dark and had attacked in the early hours of the morning. It was a strangely unpleasant feeling lying comfortably on a camp-bed, warm between the blankets, picturing one's friends advancing into a hail of shells and bullets and wondering who would be among the inevitable casualties. The quartermaster was lying the other side of the tent. I knew he wasn't asleep either, but I did not let on that I knew. On these occasions he always pretended to be the hardened old soldier who didn't care a damn, and all evening he had been very irritable, but I knew well enough that he was worrying to death about all the boys to whom he had spoken so sharply on any occasion they had tried to win anything out of him. I knew that when the first casualty returns came in he would be the first to grab them, and that he would feel the losses more deeply than any of us. Neither of us slept much that night, and early in the morning the transport officer came back. His face was lined with strain and tiredness, though he was just joking about how he had not stopped to ask how things were going but had dumped his loads and raced back as hard as he could. He told us how scared he had been and how he had dodged " going in " himself whenever he could. I knew that all this nonsense was to avoid letting the quartermaster know who the casualties were. We all knew him for one of the coolest, most conscientious officers in the battalion, and one had only to look at his face to see that he had not stopped for a minute all night. I strolled out of the tent, and he joined me shortly. " Well, who are they ? " I asked quietly. He replied just as quietly, " Signal officer, carrier officer, and carrier second-in-command killed," and then gave a list of others he knew were killed or wounded. " Don't tell the quartermaster," he added ; " there may be some mistake, and it's no use worrying him unnecessarily." I nodded and asked how the battle was going. " We are over the anti-tank ditch," he replied, " but when I left the enemy were counter-attacking strongly. It will be tough going." Then he was off again, good-naturedly cursing his drivers for being so quick in loading up, so that he had to get back into it again so soon. God help those drivers, I thought, if they had not been ready for him.

I was glad to get off that day to the N.A.A.F.I. It took my mind off the fellows in the fighting. It was nearly a hundred miles back to Ben Gardane, and I raced along the road trying to get there before dark. The road was packed with trucks all moving up to the front loaded with ammunition and stores, but the road back was almost clear. Behind me in the distance I could hear the guns booming, and wave after wave of bombers flew over towards the enemy.

In spite of driving like a madman, I was fifteen miles from Ben Gardane when it became too dark to continue driving. I pulled in at a R.A.S.C. camp, and my driver and I slept the night beside our truck. In the morning I listened to the news on the R.A.S.C. officers' wireless. There was nothing to tell me how things were going, just " Our forces are attacking and heavy fighting is in progress." I wondered if the people at home who were hearing that realised what it really meant. I did not think they did. I could imagine many I knew switching on for the headlines and remarking over their breakfast,

"The Eighth are at it again—soon be in Tunis now." And then they would turn their minds to their own little affairs, which seemed so much more important. Some would care, though: those who had sons and husbands out there would be listening with a sickening feeling in their stomach. "I wonder if he is in it. Oh, I do hope he is safe."

I jumped back into the truck, and off we went again. I drove into the transit camp in time for breakfast, and then moved over to the N.A.A.F.I. I was informed by a sergeant that the store would not be open for another three hours. I knew the journey back would be slow, and I was anxious to get back before dark. The men were very short of cigarettes, and after a battle was the time when they most needed them. I went over to the officer's tent. He was still in bed, and not at all pleased to see me. "You will have to wait for the proper time; I can't serve you now; come back in the afternoon." Controlling my rising temper I pointed out that I had come a hundred miles and had to get back before dark, and that the men were now in the middle of a battle and would be desperate for fags when it was over. It meant absolutely nothing to him, and he answered rudely, "Three o'clock this afternoon." There was nothing I could do about it. I knew he was strictly within his rights, so muttering "You insolent swine," I returned to the sergeant. He was already serving people, and quickly I slipped into the queue. He raised his eyebrows when my turn came, but presuming I suppose that I had his officer's permission, he served me, and I was able to start back by noon.

It was late in the afternoon when I began to approach the battle-zone. The guns were silent, and I knew that the battle must be over. I was desperately impatient to get back and find out, and the trucks ahead were maddeningly slow. Then I saw a welcome sight: truck-load after truck-load of German and Italian prisoners passed me in a never-ending stream. Usually the Germans and Italians were in separate trucks, but where they were in the same truck, however crowded it was, there was a gap between the Germans and Italians. The Axis partners were as friendly as cats and dogs! The Italians looked tired but happy. The Germans were sullen, and scowled at the cheery calls from our troops who were passing on their way up the line.

I learnt that "B" echelon had already moved up beyond Gabes and that our troops were through and well beyond the town. The battle had gone on well into the night, and then just before dawn the enemy had pulled out and retreated to Sfax. Already our battalion was half-way to Sfax in hot pursuit. I caught up with "B" echelon camped at the side of the road. I had had to pass through the battlefield along narrow tracks which had been made through the minefields. The salvage and burial squads had not yet arrived, and the scene was one of utter desolation. Bodies lay about where they had fallen; half-destroyed guns and burnt-out tanks were strewn about in utter confusion. Already the sweet, sickly smell of death was thick in the air, and I breathed a sigh of relief when we were finally through and on the main road. Prisoners were still pouring back in endless columns to the P.O.W. cages. The Germans were a tired, dispirited lot, some of whom raised their eyes to look with listless curiosity at the crowded trucks of Jocks which poured in a never-ending stream along the well-built road. We passed small groups of Italians who were trudging wearily along the road to give themselves up. They would go up to any officer or N.C.O. they could see and try to surrender, and would be brusquely ordered to carry on down the road unguarded and ignored.

The next morning we started early to catch up the battalion. News had come through that Sfax had fallen, and our troops were already half-way to Sousse. It looked as if all organised resistance had been broken, and we had visions of driving straight into Tunis. We passed for the first time groups of Americans who had come up from the south a few weeks before and had been attempting to drive into Gafsa. We stopped for breakfast by the roadside, and here occurred one of those tragedies of war which, because they happen outside the heat of battle, always seem so much worse. Our brigade supply officer was having breakfast leaning against a tree. I stopped to speak to him, and then jumping back into my truck started to drive to a point a hundred yards farther up the road, where he told me that our " B " echelon H.Q. was. I had hardly left him when there was a loud explosion. I saw people running. Somehow I didn't connect the explosion with him, and, anxious to get my truck off the road to clear the way for the traffic going through, I carried on. When I arrived at " B " echelon H.Q. I saw a group staring back along the road, and the quartermaster said, " I think a mine has just gone off." A truck raced up, and soon an ambulance came racing up. I went across, and found that the supply officer's batman, in the process of handing him his breakfast, had stepped on a mine, killing his officer and seriously wounding himself. This incident cast a gloom over us all and damped our high spirits, but so resilient are one's feelings in war that within an hour, when we were on the road again, we had almost forgotten about it. The road was littered with enemy trucks and guns, which had been hastily pushed to the sides. Every bridge or bend in the road had a destroyed gun or tank, where the enemy had tried desperately to hold up our advance to give their main body time to get away. We drove all day, and caught up with the battalion some twenty miles from Sfax. Other units had gone through us, and we had been pulled out for a rest and reorganisation. Our casualties had been heavy, though fortunately mainly in wounded. The following day we made our way in a more leisurely fashion to a camp site just beyond Sfax, and that night I rejoined the battalion.

## CHAPTER XVII.

### RESTING IN SFAX.

It was good to be back in harness again; there had been too little to do and therefore too much time for thinking during my fortnight at "B" echelon, and particularly during the last days. I had become very restless. The company commander was among the wounded, and I once more took over the company. The first company parade gave me rather a shock. There were many old faces missing, and as I went round the ranks inquiring about the men I had got to know so well during the advance on Tripoli and the early days in the Mareth Line, I became very depressed at the numbers I learnt would never be back again.

There was a lot of work to be done, however, and at first I had only one officer to help me, and he was wounded in the ankle. Men had to be refitted, records had to be brought up to date, relatives had to be notified of casualties, and, of course, the ordinary routine of company training and drill was restarted immediately. There is nothing worse for morale after a big engagement than to give men too much time on their hands. Sports and swimming parties were organised, and new men soon arrived and had to be absorbed into freshly organised platoons. After the first few days it was decided to combine two of the companies; and the spare company commander, thus made available, was transferred to my company. This was a great help, and it was not long before the company was once more on its feet and ready for the next show.

They were good days too. We used to sit up late at night in the Italian tent, which we had still managed to retain in our stores, and we would talk for hours over the newly arrived and accumulated ration of whisky and gin. We devised all kinds of concoctions to go with the gin, from locally procured lemons to watered-down tomato sauce. Some nights we would invite officers over from other companies to play bridge, and the games would sometimes continue almost to first light next morning. Brigade H.Q. held a garden-party, to which some of the local French officials were invited. The combined pipes and drums of the brigade played, and we stood round talking and drinking tea and eating sandwiches as if the war had never existed.

Sfax was badly smashed up and there was not much life left in it. Most of the French families had sought refuge in Algeria, and the majority of those left were not very friendly towards us. The few that were, tried hard to make up for it, but the tendency among the French residents was to complain that we were as much responsible for their present miseries as the Germans. They claimed that by refusing to acknowledge that we were " beaten " in 1940 we had prolonged the war and brought untold miseries on millions of innocent people. This was a complaint and an attitude which we were to meet over and over again during the next few months while we were in French territory, and it hurt and puzzled us. It was not that these people were pro-German, though there were some who were, but that they could not or would not face the larger issues of the war, and considered it only in the light of their own suffering and that of France itself. It was the same attitude which I suppose was the cause of the sudden collapse in France in 1940. These people lived for the present only, and the present had been made more uncomfortable than ever by the R.A.F.'s bombing of their town, and they did not wish to consider whether this was a necessary prelude to freeing it from German rule. The Germans had been a nuisance and sometimes worse, but at least they had then had their homes intact even if they had to share them with German soldiers, whereas now many of them had no homes and others had their windows smashed in. The Germans, too, had created an artificial prosperity by buying up everything and anything of value, while our troops had little or nothing to spend, and when they did buy anything they argued about the prices charged. (*Note.*—The Germans had used occupation marks and metropolitan French francs, and as they controlled the French banks they could print as much as they wished. The Allied authorities had come to an agreement with the local French authorities by which the rate of exchange was pegged at 200 francs to the £. The original rate had been 300 francs to the £, and even that rate was highly favourable to the French, as the purchasing value of the franc was practically nil. Even the smallest articles, when available at all, were beyond the purses of our soldiers.)

The Germans, too, had manipulated rationing in such a way that collaborators or near collaborators were hardly affected, while the rest of the population were left on the verge of starvation with worthless ration cards. Even this system was on the point of breaking down when we arrived, and as the Germans had taken away or destroyed all stores of food-stuff the situation was critical. The recent collaborators were chiefly the official classes, and it was natural that they were more in a position to make their complaints heard. Sometimes, too, the British troops unwittingly stirred up resentment. Being so used to being robbed and exploited by the Arabs and having so recently come from an occupied enemy country, they did not always differentiate between the attitude necessary for dealings with enemy people and a " friendly liberated people."

After the first attempt we did not mix with the local people, and accepted the situation for what it was.

Meanwhile the chase had gone steadily on. Sousse had fallen, and already the vanguard of the Eighth Army had reached Enfideville and the foot of the mountains surrounding Tunis. In these days we heard little of the doings of the First Army, and I am afraid that most of us looked upon it as a force that might be useful in containing the enemy and forcing Rommel to fight it out with us to the finish. Some of our more gloomy prophets even went so far as to suggest that Rommel might break his way through the First Army and escape into Algeria, where we should have hell's own job to dig him out of the mountains. It was only when we arrived up at Enfidaville that we realised what the First Army had been up against, and it was then that we learnt with amazement what a small force it was. An army in name only. When we saw the country and realised the difficulties they had been up against, any feelings of superiority we might have had were engulfed in our appreciation and admiration for this splendid little army, which had fought so grimly throughout the winter months.

At the end of a fortnight we were re-equipped, reinforced, and rested and ready for action again, and the order came to move forward to the Enfidaville area.

# CHAPTER XVIII.

### ENFIDAVILLE AND THE END OF THE CAMPAIGN.

WE set off in trucks early in the morning. At first we kept to the main road, travelling at speed to Sousse. We began to pass Yankee working-parties busily engaged on repairing bridges and telephone lines. There was a good deal of banter between our Jocks and the Americans, and sometimes I'm afraid there was a little sharpness from some of our tongues, but on the whole it was taken in good part. Whenever we stopped, groups of these Americans would come up to the trucks and offer fabulous prices for battle souvenirs. They seemed to have limitless dollars and francs, and even a row of Italian medals (which are two-a-penny on every Italian soldier) would fetch £2 or £3. German Luger pistols would sell at £12 to £15 each, and our Jocks, who in spite of the limited space they have available for carrying even the most necessary kits, always seemed to be able to produce any articles asked for.

We by-passed Sousse, and finally arrived at a sector of the front north of Enfidaville, just as it was becoming dark. Here we took over from the Indians on a quiet sector. The forward positions were dug out on a plain which stretched for about one and a half miles to the foot of a mountain range. To our right and well forward of the range was a rocky mountain with an Arab village perched precariously on the top. This had just been taken from the Germans by the New Zealanders, who had had to fight their way by foot up the sheer mountain-side. It was vital for us that the Germans were driven off, for while they held it they could overlook the road leading to Enfidaville and the country for miles round. The mountains in front of us stretched away to the left as far as the eye could see. Those immediately in front of us were occupied by the enemy, who had dug themselves into almost impregnable positions from which they could overlook the whole plain, but those to the left were already in our hands. The night we moved in we witnessed an attack in which our troops advanced one mountain farther to the right. It was an unusual position, for we were facing a front half of which was in our hands and half in enemy hands, and it was as if we were spectators on the touch-line of a football field. We would watch the shelling and counter-shelling, and then suddenly the enemy gunners would turn their attention to us and lob a few shells into our midst as if they wished to impress on us that they had not forgotten we were there.

During the following days we had to lie still in our holes throughout the day, unable to move about for any purpose. At night we strengthened our defences and laid minefields, the enemy occasionally sending over bursts of machine-gun fire to harry us. We made one or two hit-and-run raids on the enemy's forward positions at the foot of the hills, rushing in quickly throwing grenades and firing tommy-guns and rushing back as quickly as we came. This kept the enemy continually on edge, and Very lights used to go up every few minutes; but on the whole it was an artillery action, and apart from the discomfort in which we lived we were left in peace. The worst of these discomforts by far were the mosquitoes. From dusk to dawn they attacked us in swarms and settled on our faces and arms, and even sucked our blood through our battle-dress jackets. We killed them by the hundreds, but they still swarmed over us. Our faces and necks were swollen with bites; sleeping at nights was almost impossible. We would lie in the bottom of our holes and cover ourselves completely with our gas-capes, but apart from the fact that we nearly suffocated, the brutes still found their way through the folds and settled on our necks and heads.

After a week of this rather miserable existence, during which we had long since read any literature we were lucky enough to get, we were reduced to passing the long hours by organising beetle-races along the walls of our trenches. These beetles were huge creatures with powerful back legs with which they pushed lumps of earth, &c., over incredible distances, sometimes climbing on top of the lumps and levering them forward with their back legs, and often, especially when coming up against obstacles, going into reverse and working their way backwards over the obstacle pushing their lumps with them. We dug channels into the walls of the trenches, and capturing four of these insects we would set them off together, encouraging them along with bits of sticks and getting as excited as an "Ascot" crowd. Soon we became more ambitious and organised "point to point," often unnecessarily exposing ourselves in our excitement and eagerness to drive on our particular "horse." A "tote" was started, and bets were carefully regulated.

It was on the ninth day that I was summoned to Battalion H.Q., where I was told that I was to be loaned to a brigade of a new division which had just come up. This brigade had taken over a sector of the front a mile or two beyond Enfidaville, and my duties were to visit the various companies and talk to them and give advice about patrols and forward positions. I felt rather diffident at first, for it is always difficult to give personal experience without appearing to be "shooting a line," but from Brigade H.Q. down to the forward platoons they were so friendly and so obviously anxious to pick up what tips they could, that I soon felt quite at home. Their greatest fault was one which all troops new to the fighting line were guilty of, failure to realise the importance of digging in and digging in deeply. Unfortunately the unit they had taken over from had done very little digging in either, and even worse, had given the impression that this was rather an old wife's habit. As a result, the new troops had suffered unnecessary casualties, and when I arrived a " blitz " had just started, to make everyone dig as hard as they could. When I heartily endorsed this policy some of the officers were quite relieved, for they had been in some doubt whether this digging was " scare stuff." I lived at Brigade H.Q., which itself was under shell-fire, quite heavy at times. Once the Officers' Mess, crowded for lunch, had a very narrow escape. I went up daily to visit the forward positions. To get up to these I had to travel along the road through Enfidaville and run the gauntlet of enemy shells which were exploding regularly along this road, and once the jeep in which I was travelling was blown right off the road by the blast from a nearby explosion. To reach one position it was necessary to cross a railway-line, which stretched along an avenue of trees absolutely straight into the enemy lines. The enemy had a machine-gun firing down this line, and used to wait until a vehicle or group of men passed over, and then let fly. Usually they were too late to hit the first vehicle or party, but if there was a second following closely behind it got the full burst of bullets. We used to dash across this railway with a hiss of bullets behind us. Altogether it was quite an exciting journey.

I spent a very happy week with this brigade. Being newly up and having come from a land of plenty, they had brought with them all sorts of luxuries in the food and drink line, and I flourished on both after long weeks of bully and biscuits and water. The relief of being able to stretch one's legs and move about during the day and the freedom from mosquitoes were worth all the additional shelling, which was not really bad anyway.

After a week here I was called back to my own battalion, and returned convinced that we were about to make an attack. I did not relish attacking those mountains, and was very sorry to leave the comparative comfort of a well-stocked Brigade H.Q. However, when I reported back I learnt to my astonishment that we were moving out and that the Free French were taking over. I learnt further that we were leaving the battle-zone altogether and moving into Algeria. I thought that this meant we were going to strengthen the First Army in their attack on Tunis. It was quite obvious that an attack from our sector would be a very expensive undertaking, and already two infantry and one armoured division of the Eighth Army had gone round to join the First Army. Meanwhile the French had been closing in from the south, and the Americans, with French support, were advancing towards Bizerta.

The final clash was imminent, and it really looked as if we had Rommel and Von Arnim too—trapped this time. However, that night I was told that I was to be in charge of the battalion advance party and that we were going to the Algerian coast to rest and reorganise and were not to be in at the final kill. At first this news cheered me and everyone else, for we were all tired out and fed up to the teeth with fighting; but as the situation became clearer, our first relief turned to anger, for we realised that after our chasing Rommel right across Africa the honour of the final capitulation was to go to the First Army, reinforced with units of the Eighth. We did not grudge the First Army Tunis, though we looked upon that also as our lawful prize, and of course they were entitled to Von Arnim; but Rommel was ours and ours only, and it only lessened the disappointment slightly to realise that there was still a large part of the Eighth Army in at the kill, even though they were serving under another army. But at the time we were far too excited at the prospects of a real rest in a country untouched by war to worry much about anything else.

That night the French took over from us, and we were amused at the way they drove right up to the forward positions with their head-lights full on. To our amazement there was scarcely any reaction from the enemy, who were to surrender *en masse* two days later. Already quite large parties were slipping out of their lines and coming over to give themselves up. The German is still a poor fighter in a losing battle, and though it had taken us a long time to convince him he was losing, when the realisation did come he broke completely. I have never seen such a wretched, demoralised crowd of men, and I learnt later that when the final surrender came they were even worse. As for the Italians, they had already degenerated into a complete rabble; but even as far back as Mareth they had given up all pretence of fighting and were just a handicap to the Germans.

## CHAPTER XIX.

### JOURNEY THROUGH ALGERIA.

I SET off the following morning with my party to join the brigade advance party. We travelled all day, making a wide sweep inland, and crossed the Algerian frontier that night. The second day we began to notice the difference. Villages and towns untouched by war, with the people, Arabs and French, going about their everyday tasks. The only signs of war were the large American camps and the crowds of American soldiers loafing about in the streets. We had seen very few Americans before, apart from the ones we had met on our way to Enfidaville, for most of the Americans were garrison troops and had remained in Algeria and Morocco, but now the American flag and signs were everywhere. American military police were on duty at village cross-roads. We saw vast canteens and soldiers' social centres. The American troops nonchalantly gave our boys huge packets of chocolate and hundreds of cigarettes; otherwise they took very little notice of us, and, unlike the ones in Tunisia, were not interested in battle souvenirs. Some of them showed a little curiosity at our " desert camouflaged " and battle-scarred trucks, and when they learnt that we were Eighth Army they came forward to shake hands and congratulate us.

As we travelled on the news spread, and the inhabitants, both French and Arab, turned out in force and cheered us through the villages, shouting " Huitième Armée—Victoire ! " and showering us with flowers and nuts. We stopped from time to time to explore villages and to have a drink at the local estaminets, and each time our truck was immediately surrounded by shouting, cheering crowds. Some old man, a local dignitary, would push his way through the crowd and then read out an address of welcome in an excited voice in which the words " une rêve, un legend, glorieuse, Victoire" would tumble over each other. The men would vie with each other to stand us drinks, while the girls would throw flowers and often embrace us. Some of the older folk would ask anxiously about relatives in Tunis, Sfax and Sousse, and were quite disappointed when we told them we did not know them. We were told the most amazing rumours. The people of Metropolitan France had risen and driven the Germans out, Turkey had declared war and had invaded Bulgaria (this last we were told over and over again by Americans and French, who both swore that it had been officially broadcast from Algiers radio). We began to change our opinion about the French and were quite surprised that night when, having stopped and camped just outside a village, we were warned by the owner of a big house on the outskirts that we had better not go into the village unarmed because the people were hostile and strongly pro-Vichy. We went in, however, and again were welcomed and stood drinks. If the warning was true the Vichyites kept well out of the way, but even during all this enthusiasm it was noticeable that we were not invited into the people's houses, and even our friend, who had warned us and on whose estate we were camped, did not ask us to come in but talked to us in the garden. He had two pretty daughters of about eighteen and sixteen years, and it was so long since we had seen well-dressed European girls that we could hardly keep our eyes off them. Perhaps this was the reason why we were not invited in!

The following day we passed through the most magnificent scenery. The road wound its way along the top edge of a huge ravine, there was only the flimsiest fence between the road edge and a sheer drop of hundreds of feet. Sometimes we passed through tunnels dug right through the base of huge rocky mountains and then over magnificent suspension bridges. I soon had a deep respect for the skill and hard work of the French colonists of the late nineteenth century and it made me wonder all the more how the French people, or at least the large number who supported the Vichy Government, were willing so tamely to hand over this great inheritance to the Germans. Surely this alone was worth fighting for. The more I saw of Algeria, and later of Morocco, the more I realised how easy it would have been for the French to carry on the struggle from their Empire after the fall of France itself, and how greatly the war could have been shortened. Quite a small force, if determined, could have held the Mareth Line in the East, while only a vast major campaign by the Germans could have made any headway in such country as this. The blowing up of a single bridge could have held up the whole might of the German Army almost indefinitely. Truly the French nation had lost its soul in 1940. In fact it was defeated from within before ever a shot had been fired. I thought bitterly of all the good fellows who had been killed in the last six months fighting to recover a country which had never needed to fall into German hands, had the people of France not resigned the government of their Empire to traitors and self-seekers. I began to understand better the terrible bitterness of De Gaulle and his followers against these Vichy traitors.

We camped another night by the roadside, and the following day we arrived at the small coast town which was to be our station for the next two months. It was a peaceful little place, but, unlike the towns in the interior, we saw once more the scars of war. The Germans came over occasionally to bomb the harbour, and the village main street had ugly gaps in it, but in spite of this, life went on quite normally. There was a large casino crowded with well-dressed Frenchmen and American officers, and the white sand beach adjoining it was the playground of happy children and grown-ups bathing and sunning themselves. It was a wonderful sight for us after months of dirt and death and misery.

After marking and sign-posting the battalion area, I went down to the town and again we were welcomed with enthusiasm, though not so fervent as in the villages and towns in the interior. We looked into the casino and were immediately introduced to its owner, who was also the Mayor of the town. He promptly invited us to join him for lunch. There were three of us, and we were rather dirty and untidy in our stained K.D. shorts and battle-dress blouses, and at first we hesitated, feeling rather embarrassed among this fashionably dressed crowd of French people and immaculately uniformed American officers. We hardly remembered how to use the vast array of knives and forks laid on the spotless tables. He saw the reason for our hesitation, and, arguing fervently that it would be a great honour to lunch with "heroes of the Eighth Army," led us over to a group sitting drinking cocktails on the wide balcony overlooking the shore. Here he introduced us to his wife and daughter and a girl friend of his daughter and two American captains who were escorting them. It was clear at once that the American escorting his daughter was very interested in her, and both Americans looked a little resentful and suspicious at our joining the party.

The Mayor went into a passionate outburst of introductions in which he extolled the virtues of the Eighth Army and proclaimed that he and his family were proud of the honour of welcoming us to their town. His wife looked flustered, but the daughter looked completely bored and made no attempt to hide it. She reminded me of the hard-faced, over-dressed, and deliberately supercilious women I remembered in the fashionable hotels of pre-war Paris, or for that matter the west end of London. She was not interested in three dirty ill-dressed Britishers, and even less interested in the war in which they had been fighting and which, as I learnt later, she considered " a frightful bore and so unnecessary." She much preferred her smart well-dressed Americans, and, turning back to them, she dismissed us as completely as if she had shown us out of the door. Her friend, however, showed more interest and informed us that her husband was a prisoner of war in Germany and she hoped we had killed every *sale* Boche we had seen. We gravely told her that we had done our best, and then, seeing that her American companion was showing signs of impatience and resentment, she turned back to him.

Meanwhile the old man was babbling on, piling praise on our heads and thrusting drink after drink into our hands. He dashed upstairs to his room and returned proudly displaying the Legion of Honour medal and two others. His daughter looked absolutely disgusted and abruptly said she was hungry and was going to start lunch even if he wasn't. He looked embarrassed and started to apologise to us for his daughter's manners, but as I was the only one who had understood what she had said, I hastily interrupted him and admired his casino. We then all walked into the dining-room and sat down. A waiter hurried over immediately, and the Mayor made a great fuss about ordering wines. We had vegetable soup, *hors-d'œuvre*, roast beef, fruit salad and ice-cream, cheese and coffee, all washed down with both red and white wine. Throughout the meal the Mayor repeated over and over again how proud he was to have us with him and how he hoped we would enjoy our stay in the town. He asked us a lot of questions about the war and about military matters which we were unable to discuss with him. His wife sat silently listening, occasionally smiling and nodding when he turned to her for confirmation of some point or other. The two girls and the Americans ignored us completely.

Towards the end of the meal other Frenchmen joined us and we overflowed on to another table, the Americans and the girls withdrawing to an adjoining one. Each time a group joined us the Mayor went through the passionate eulogy of our Army's virtues until we knew it off by heart. More and more white wine appeared; it seemed very mild and apparently had no effect, but I noticed with surprise that the Frenchmen were watering it down from large jugs of iced water. It seemed to me wicked to ruin good wine like this, and I did not follow their example. After the meal was finally over we sat on talking. The other two officers, who scarcely spoke French, feeling bored, made excuses and departed; then, before I realised what was happening, the old man was up on his feet shouting to all that he was now going to call on "his good friend and hero of the Eighth Army" to address them. I realised my danger too late; there was no escape without insulting these sensitive people for all time; fortunately I was well fortified with the wine by this time, so much so that when I rose to speak the whole assembly swayed in front of my eyes. I made a desperate effort to collect my thoughts in a rather fuddled brain. I remember suddenly realising why the others had all watered their wine. The innocuous stuff, which had seemed no stronger than lemonade, was in reality stronger than anything I had ever tasted before. Fortunately I always find that alcohol improves my vocabulary in a foreign language, if not my diction. I remember trying to put a lot of feeling into my expressions of gratitude, though I cannot now remember a word I said. Somehow I got through it, there was a lot of applause, and then I was back in my seat. Now the room was going round and round with a vengeance. Some of the people were getting up to go. I wondered if I dared risk standing up; I made another supreme effort to pull myself together. I got up and very unsteadily bowed and said "Au revoir" to madame; then I turned to shake hands with the Mayor; he started to escort me to the door. I began to turn back for my balmoral, but found it had somehow already found its way into my hands. I felt I must make some remark to excuse myself. I murmured something about the wine being much stronger than I had realised; the Mayor replied that it was the heat! I stumbled into my waiting truck, shook hands with the Mayor, and before the truck was out of sight of the casino I was unconscious.

I woke in my bivy five hours later. My batman was shaking me and repeating something over and over again. At last it sank in. "The battalion is arriving, sir; you'll need to get up. There's cold water outside, sir; you'll be O.K. if you stick your head in the bucket." My head felt as if it would burst; I staggered out and held my head under the water until I nearly stopped breathing. Gradually I began to feel better. "Mac," I said, " 'ware the local ' vino ' ; it's 100 per cent red biddy." " Yes, sir," he agreed, looking me over anxiously. " Are you O.K. to meet the commanding officer ? " I nodded doubtfully, and after he had checked me over in his imperturbable way, I set off to meet the battalion coming in.

That night several of the officers went down to the casino, and, in spite of my warnings, many of them were caught out. " Water the wine indeed," they said scathingly, but the next morning it was I who was laughing. I felt rather sheepish the next time I met the Mayor, but he was at great pains to tell me how much everybody had appreciated my speech. " Could they understand me ? " I asked. " Oh yes," he replied gravely, " you never hesitated once during the whole ten minutes you spoke." " Ten minutes ? " I said with horror. " Why, yes," he replied, " it was superb." I left it at that, feeling it was wiser not to probe the details any further.

## CHAPTER XX.

### TRAINING FOR SEA INVASION.

ONCE more the promised holiday did not materialise! Within two days of the battalion's arrival we were once more in the throes of all-day training. An attempt was made to give us a " free day " once a week, but as this was organised on a battalion basis, without reference to brigade or divisional programmes, this day was almost invariably chosen for a brigade or divisional exercise. The troops, however, took it with surprising good humour; I think by this time they had ceased to expect anything different. Moreover, we did have some spare time in the evenings, and the authorities had gone to far greater pains than at Tripoli to provide entertainments and amusements.

To most of the older ones who had been through the campaign, the new training consisting of charging in and out of assault boats was a form of amusement, while those who joined us from drafts sent out from home found everything they saw fresh and diverting, and the hours of training much shorter than they had been accustomed to at home. There were other compensating factors too; we now came under the administration of the First Army with all its advantages of supply. We now got real British cigarettes—Players, Capstan, &c.— and as many as we wanted too. After months of existing on " V's " and other poor types, and these usually in short supply, this was a real treat. We got weekly rations of chocolate (we had almost forgotten what it tasted like), and even sweets, but greatest luxury of all was the ordinary daily rations. Real bread instead of the brick-hard biscuits. Spam instead of the everlasting bully. Real margarine instead of the fat substitute issued in the desert, and fresh meat and vegetables from time to time. Sugar, tea, and all the other daily items were now more plentiful. Meals were once more a pleasure instead of being a matter of keeping the stomach supplied. I remember our shocked horror the first time we heard some First Army troops complaining about the spam and the fact that the bread was a little stale. It was also possible to get quite a good meal in the town, including that fast favourite of all Tommies, " chips " wrapped in a newspaper, even though the latter was not the ' Noon Record ' with the latest racing results.

Yes, life was good for us all at D———. The people on the whole were friendly. There were attractively dressed girls, many of whom invited the Jocks into their houses to meet their families, and, even when the Jocks found that Marie Louise brought Pa, Ma, and even big brother with her every time they invited her to go to the pictures with them, it did not altogether damp their enthusiasm even if it made big inroads into their accumulated pay. The training on the beaches, too, soon developed into a game, and an impromptu bathing parade, and an attempt by some newly imported training officers to make it more realistic by the use of live grenades, soon stopped when the Jocks, who had had enough of that sort of thing in real actions, threw the grenades back at the instructors, their officers meanwhile looking the other way. These instructors, fresh from home battle schools, soon learnt to differentiate between the veterans and the newly arrived reinforcements, with the result that the former soon found that they had plenty of spare time. All ranks were catered for, and no officious Catering Corps majors came to turn the officers out of the casino. The staff wallahs were miles away and left us in peace.

We had many cheery parties and organised dinners. We became friendly with the American officers, who used a part of the casino as a Rest House. They invited us into their rooms, where we held uproarious sing-songs. We learnt about the feuds between Yankees and Confederates, and always took the part of the latter, just as the Confederate always took the part of the Scots in Scots *versus* English " battles." We learnt their songs and they learnt ours. Soon they were coming up to our Mess, and one Sunday an American padre took the Camp Service. Even the two who had eyed us askance the first day relaxed and joined in the fun when they were sure we were not going to " crash in " on their girls.

The old Mayor invited our senior officers to dinner, and we returned the compliment in our Mess. We had one particularly uproarious Guest Night to celebrate our late commanding officer (who had recently left us to command a brigade) winning the V.C. Our P.M.C. scoured the country for miles around, and produced a dinner that excelled any that we had ever had even in pre-war days.

There was a very nice family living in a farm adjoining our camp. It consisted of grandpapa, mother and two sweet children, Paul aged ten, and Jeanne-Hugh aged eight. The father was an Englishman serving in the British Navy. Grandpapa and mother were French. Grandpapa had come out to Algiers in the eighties, and had built the farm and developed the adjoining ground into a fine estate which produced almost everything the country could grow. They were staunch De Gaullists and could not do enough for us. Sometimes a few of us would go up to the farm in the evening and play with the children and help with the haymaking. Paul spoke perfect English and used to give me lessons in French. He was a sharp laddie, and would not hesitate to correct me if, when talking to his mother or her friends, I made some mistake in grammar. Through his teaching my French improved 100 per cent. His little sister, whose double-barrelled name was a combination of her mother's and father's names, could not speak a word of English, and was very shy at first. My company cooks had found and adopted a dog left by the Germans during their retreat from Mareth. The dog had an elaborate collar with its late owner's name on it and also its own name, " Rommel." When the order came that all pets—and there were many in the camp—had to be disposed of, I persuaded the cook to give the dog to Paul. Almost at once the boy and the dog became inseparable pals, Rommel trotting along behind Paul wherever he went. He used to come down to my bivy in the early morning with a bottle of fresh milk and two eggs, which I would take into breakfast with me. Several times I was invited to dinner at the farm, Paul coming running down excitedly with the invitation. We would sit round a table on the balcony in the cool of the evening, and, gazing over the well-kept fields and allotments, it was easy to imagine oneself back at home.

I shall never forget those peaceful evenings. The war was far away, and leaning back contentedly in my chair after a sumptuous dinner of roast duck and fresh vegetables, fruit and cream with fine wines and liqueurs, it was difficult to imagine that I had ever taken part in it. When the meal was cleared away the conversation invariably turned to politics. The old man lived in the past glories of France. He was a staunch follower of the last Emperor Napoleon III., and was very bitter about the rabble of vulgar self-seekers who had brought France to her present disaster. He had visions, I think, of De Gaulle becoming emperor of a new and purged France. He had violently resisted the regulations imposed by the German-Italian Armistice Commission, and only his age and the respect in which he was held throughout the district had saved him from being arrested by the Vichy authorities prior to the British landings. They had all been confined to their estate, and much of their stock and produce had been confiscated. He spoke bitterly about the old Mayor, who, he said, was a traitor and a turncoat, who had been foremost in collaborating with the Commission. He had enlisted as a youth in the last days of the Franco-Prussian War, and hated the Germans with a hatred that knew no limits.

Frequently we used to have German air raids directed on the harbour, which was packed with invasion craft, and while the rest of the family went into the shelter he would stand in front of his door waving his stick in the air, and shouting, " Sale Boche ! " at the top of his voice. The shrapnel from the A.A. guns would fall all round him, but he did not even notice it. Some of these raids were quite bad, and the camp and farm, though well inland, received some very near misses. He was puzzled and annoyed at the continual bickering between the De Gaullists and Giraudists, which by this time was coming increasingly into the open. He would pick up the local paper and start to read it, suddenly flinging it down and shouting, " Imbeciles ; why cannot they settle their differences and concentrate on the Boche ? " He admired Giraud as representing the best element of the French Regular Army, but De Gaulle was his hero and could do no wrong. He wrote strong letters to the Press, and stormed and fumed when they were not printed. He had no use for Democracy as far as France was concerned. French people, he said, required firm governing parliaments, and political debates did not suit their temperament and only led to violent quarrelling. French politics were rotten to the core, and no decent Frenchman would have anything to do with them.

I pointed out that this appeared to me to be the reason why France had fallen so low ; surely it was the duty of decent Frenchmen to take up politics and thereby govern the country soundly. He shook his head vehemently and replied, " No, it was discipline that France needed." It was so different in Britain. The British were so law-abiding and so patriotic and unified, and that was mainly because they had a King. I reminded him that British politics had sunk pretty low before the war, and he interrupted excitedly, saying, " Ah, but your people were sound, only lazy." Perhaps, I admitted, but many of us wondered if even our country would not have produced its crop of quislings and collaborators if the Germans had succeeded in invading us in 1940. I added that sometimes I almost wished they had, so that we could have found out who was true and who was not. When he referred to Oswald Mosley and his Fascists, I replied that I did not consider these men really dangerous, and that they probably would have done more good to the British war effort if they had been released and allowed to shout their slogans in Hyde Park. He could not understand this, and said they should have been shot long ago. I started to try and explain the ordinary Britisher's reactions to all extremists, but I saw he didn't understand.

I changed the subject and asked him what he thought would happen to France after the war. He replied that it depended a great deal on British policy towards Germany, but he also feared that there would be considerable dislike and jealousy of Britain on the part of many Frenchmen born of shame that they had not continued the fight in 1940. Already, he said, there were many who continued to support the Vichy régime for this reason only. He thought it would require all the tact and understanding that the British could muster to combat this feeling. Unfortunately the British were not endowed with either of these qualities. I agreed, and went on to tell him of our unpleasant experiences with the French people in Tunisia. He nodded glumly and said he had expected as much, then violently again he shouted, " You will be soft with the Germans ; I know it ; you are always more friendly with your enemies after a war than with your friends."

I smiled, and reminded him that this time our own country had suffered ; whole towns had been ravaged by bombs.

" But you can't hate," he replied. " You will not destroy their women so that no more Germans can be born." I agreed, and replied that even if that were wise it was impossible to destroy a whole nation. What was needed was a firm but just rule of the German nation for a whole generation. I did not think we would " lend " the Germans the money with which to prepare a fresh war this time, but that that was the danger I feared most when I referred to our own near collaborators. We, the ordinary people, had not forgotten the disgraceful crime of handing over to the Germans half of our " Munich apology money" which we had given to the Czechs. I did not think that some of those responsible realised how strongly the ordinary people felt about that action, which seemed to some of us as bad as any action by the quislings of the Continent.

I had many similar talks with the old man, and always he reiterated that France could only rise again under what amounted to a military dictatorship. I could not agree with him, but I admired his passionate patriotism and love of France. These talks would go on late into the night, until finally interrupted either by an air raid or by madam firmly ordering the old man to bed, while I humbly apologised for outstaying my welcome.

I enjoyed these evenings, which I alternated with parties at the casino or in the Mess. When the time came to say good-bye I do not know who was most upset at the parting, but I shall never forget this French family's kindness, and I treasure the parting gift of the children—a Lorraine cross brooch and a photo of little Paul.

Towards the end of our stay at D—— I left the battalion to take up an appointment at Brigade as transport officer. My leg wounds were still troubling me and would not stand up to the marching, and particularly the climbing of cliffs, which was the basis of our training. I was very sorry to leave the battalion in which I had served since the old care-free Territorial Army days, but it was an interesting job I was taking up, and one which would require all my energies in the forthcoming action. It also gave me a chance to rest my legs for the first time since I had rejoined the battalion at Sfax.

Invasion preparations were now well advanced, it was the last week in June, but none of us, not even the commanding officers, knew where the invasion was taking place. Each command was issued with a section of map covering his own sector, from which all names had been removed. It was not permitted to compare sectors. When we studied the pending action on sand table models, each small unit was taken separately. It was also forbidden to discuss the matter among ourselves. The directing staff even went to the extent of leaving operational maps of places like Crete or Greece deliberately lying about to throw the inquisitive further off the scent and at the same time trace rumour-mongers by the resultant rumours which followed the finding of these false maps. About this time two Greek officers were attached to Brigade H.Q., and of course everyone began to leap to conclusions.

We moved from our pleasant camps along the Algerian coast back to the dreary desert, dried-up olive groves and stinking Arab villages of Tunisia. I was responsible for the waterproofing of all vehicles in the Brigade group and the separating of them into some hundred serials for loading purposes. Huge vehicle parks had been established by R.E.M.E., and into the bays in these parks vehicles of all types from huge Sherman tanks to jeeps poured in never-ending streams from dawn to dusk. Groups of perspiring mechanics adapted and waterproofed vehicle after vehicle while the blazing midsummer African sun beat down mercilessly on their naked backs. The sand tracks leading up to the various bays were continually churned up by the passing vehicles, until the air was so thick with fine particles of sand that it was impossible to see the bonnet of one's truck from the driver's seat. Huge piles of waterproofing material lay alongside the bays, and tons of this material must have been used during the fortnight preceding the invasion.

Serials were called for from units in sequence, and sometimes bottle-necks were created by units failing to send their serials at the proper time. On other occasions whole routes were blocked for miles because serials had been sent incomplete, and were therefore held up in the bays which were required for fresh vehicles. But considering the size of the task and that it was unique in the history of war, the work went on with precision and efficiency. Dashing from bay to bay, phoning to units for lost vehicles or serials, dashing down to the docks to check up the loading, my days passed like minutes. There was no time to return for meals. I just ate a biscuit and drank lukewarm water from a water-bottle while on the job.

Occasionally tempers got frayed when two units claimed

the same bay at the same time, and differences had to be smoothed out by improvisation. The worst problem was the congestion on the roads and tracks, and over and over again I had to dash along the side of the roads in my jeep, bumping over the rough verge, to sort out and extricate serials jammed in a solid mass of vehicles.

As the days passed the congestion lessened, and ship after ship reported load complete. I was dead tired by night, for the heat and the sand, which one could not help breathing in, took more out of one than a long march. Sometimes it was difficult to be polite when commanding officers telephoned complaining bitterly about this or that serial being held up. Nearly always such hold-ups were due to the units concerned not having kept to the instructions issued, but everyone was keyed up and the heat was hellish, and allowances had to be made. Sometimes it was necessary to work far into the night preparing and checking lists of vehicles loaded. To make matters worse, one of my leg wounds chose this time to start festering. I had not time to have it attended to, and soon it had swollen up and throbbed agonisingly as I dashed from place to place. When I finally found time to see a doctor I was told I would have to go into hospital for treatment. It was impossible to go then, but as I had been detailed to stay behind with the " B " echelon vehicles, which were not going over till the beach-heads had been firmly established, I decided to hold on till the first wave had gone.

One day towards the end of this period of preparation I called in to see some of my friends in the battalion. I had a long talk with a particular friend of mine, and we discussed the prospects of getting home after this next show was over. It was the last time I was to speak to him, together with many others of the old crowd ; he was killed at the battle of Gerbini, near Catania.

It was during this period, too, that we had a visit from the famous Scots comedian Will Fyfe. Praying that all would go well in my absence, I took an evening off to hear him sing to the troops. I would not have missed him for anything. Every Jock that could be spared was packed round the stage, which consisted of two three-tonner trucks. Perspiring with the heat, and with his arms and face peeling from the scorching sun, Will sang all the old favourites and acted all his well-known turns, but the roar that went up when he started " I belong to Glesca " must have been heard back home. Encore after encore was demanded, and poor Will, who already had given two shows that day besides driving many miles along the dust-drenched sand-tracks, grinned cheerfully and obliged till his voice was cracking.

He had dinner in the Brigade Mess that night. How I longed to take him over to our Battalion Mess! A Brigade H.Q. Mess, made up as it is of specialist officers of all branches of the Services, is always inclined to be sticky and formal. That night it appeared to excel itself in formality; poor old Will only got two small nips, and when he tried to liven the proceedings with a song only a few voices joined in, in a quiet genteel way. I saw him wince every time he was addressed as Mr Fyfe, and I knew he was longing for a real party with the boys. He made a friendly speech in which he gave us a message from the folks at home, and even this was only replied to by a formal clapping of hands. I kept imagining the party we would have had in the battalion. The doctor would have given his famous imitation of Will Fyfe's contemporary Dave Willis, and " D " company commander would have had " the Division on Parade," a friendly burlesque of our divisional commander. Drinks would have been flowing and everyone would have sung at the top of their voices. There he would have been just " Will "—the Jocks' friend.

I was on the verge of defying etiquette and asking him to come over with me, when he rose to go. He asked if he could sing one more song to the boys before he left, and I thought I understood the reason. He wanted his last impression to be one of true Scots enthusiasm, and he wanted to wipe out the memory of this cold formal party. The senior officers, of course, were up to their eyes in work and were in no way responsible for this fiasco—in fact they were the cheeriest members of the party—but on that occasion the junior officers, who were in a large majority, were the tamest crowd I had ever met. I knew from that day on that I could never stick that Mess, and I was determined to get back to the battalion at the earliest opportunity.

The next day was Sunday. We had a church parade, and the divisional commander spoke to us afterwards. We knew the day was approaching. Two days later I stood watching my own battalion marching off to embark; it was the last time I was to see many of the faces I knew so well. After they had passed I packed my things and made my way to the hospital.

The next day I had another piece of shrapnel removed and the abscess around it treated.

## CHAPTER XXI.

FOLLOWING THE SICILY CAMPAIGN FROM AN AFRICAN BASE.

For the next four days I awoke at seven o'clock each morning to listen to the news, and on the fifth morning the long-awaited announcement came: " British, Canadian, and American troops landed on Sicily in the early hours of this morning. The beach defences were overwhelmed and the troops are now pushing inland. We hope to give further details in our next bulletin."

So it was Sicily after all! After that I listened eagerly to every bulletin.

The following day the first casualties began to arrive; they were all Canadians who had been wounded in the initial landings and could give me little or no news of what was happening. The B.B.C. was tantalisingly vague. The days passed and each day brought fresh casualties, but they were all from different sectors from that of my own division. They all agreed that the real fight was still to come; the beaches had been half-heartedly defended by Italians, who were showing even less interest in the war than they had during the latter stages of the Tunisian campaign. This was interesting, for it had been argued that the Italians, who didn't care for their African possessions, would fight bitterly if their own country was attacked. Now it was clear that they had had enough: they only wanted peace—" peace at any price."

We had Italian prisoners as attendants in the hospital, and they too showed nothing but delight when we told them that the Allies were pushing rapidly inland. " It will be all finished soon and we shall be able to return home; you Inglese must push on quick, quick before the Tedeschi (Germans) replace the Italian garrisons." They showed no feelings of shame or humiliation or hatred for the enemy they had sworn to " wipe from the fair face of Africa."

Towards the end of July I left the hospital and rejoined the brigade " B " echelon, which was still in Africa. By this time all the fighting-line vehicles of the brigade had been trans-shipped to Sicily and only the heavy store vehicles remained. There was very little to do until " B " echelon was called for, and I spent the time mainly in sight-seeing. I visited Tunis and the nearby ancient ruins of Carthage. The latter were very disappointing, just a few half-unearthed chunks of stone which might have been an old graveyard, but I suppose they would mean more to an archæologist.

Tunis was beginning to come back to life ; the hotels were doing a roaring trade with the Americans ; there were very few British troops there, but thousands of Americans. One could get quite a good meal, but drinks were confined to two or three local wines of indifferent quality. Prices, of course, were scandalous. Rubbishy trinkets of a kind of white metal, which the merchants claimed was silver, were offered at £3 or £4. A bottle of wine, which if sold at all before our occupation would have cost 2s., now cost 12s. to 15s. Most of the shops were owned by Jews or Italians, but Frenchmen, Italians, Arabs, and Jews all vied with each other to exploit the soldiers to the utmost. The shopping section of the town was almost untouched by bombs, but the harbour area was pretty badly smashed up.

There were two picture-houses open, one showing "Desert Victory" and the other an American film. There were huge queues outside both. I finally got into the picture-house showing "Desert Victory." It was quite a good propaganda film, I suppose, for those who knew no better, but I could not help thinking that the Russians and Americans would have made a better job of it. Many of the " battle scenes " showed clearly that they were taken at the training depot with immaculately dressed depot troops attacking " German " positions, during which the only casualties seen were German. The impression one got, and one which I have since learnt is very general at home, was that after Alamein we simply got into trucks and drove to Tripoli, where we marched in triumphant ceremony with flags flying and bands playing, to be greeted by Winston Churchill, who had apparently arrived there before us. The early scenes prior to the battle and the impression of the barrage at Alamein were good, but the scenes of infantry attacks were laughable.

There was little to do in Tunis; it was a poorer edition of Cairo and a slightly better edition of Tripoli. On other days I visited the battlefields round Enfidaville. It was particularly interesting to climb up to the enemy positions in the hills and look across our own lines. They were ideal defensive positions, and I should imagine the answer to any artillery officer's prayer. I suppose they had been short of artillery, for from those positions they could have blasted us to hell with perfect direct observation. The Graves Commission had not yet completed its work in the enemy area and there were still many unpleasant sights lying about. In one place some Italian soldiers who had been hastily buried had been dug up again by the Arabs, who had stripped them of their boots and clothing. There was a dead and eerie silence throughout this vast area which had been so recently teeming with thousands of men. It was still necessary to tread warily to avoid the mines, and once I nearly came to grief when I drove my jeep along a track which suddenly ended in the middle of a minefield. I picked up a fine pair of German binoculars which I found lying in front of an old observation post. I wandered back into the dugouts we had occupied; some of the old papers and magazines I had been reading when I was called out to go to the newly arrived division were still lying there. The channel in the trench wall which we had used for our beetle-races was still intact. It was becoming dusk and I heard an angry buzz of a mosquito and hastily jumped back into my jeep and returned to the camp.

Early in August some of our own lightly wounded came back to us and we got the first authentic news of the battalion. The B.B.C. was reporting fierce fighting around Catania, and for over a week there had been no progress reported on this front. Now we heard that there had been a ferocious battle around the Gerbini airfield. My battalion had been in the thick of it and casualties had been heavy. Two of my best friends had been killed among many others, including our new commanding officer. This had happened over a week ago, but it was the first time we had heard of it, so completely were we cut off from those in Sicily. It was hard to believe at first that so many friends whom I had said good-bye to that morning the battalion marched off to embark, would never be seen again. When one is in battle with them one does not feel the loss so much as when one hears it in this manner. I was beginning to get restless at the delay in getting over, and after hearing this news I moved heaven and earth to obtain ships to take us over.

## CHAPTER XXII.

### LANDING IN SICILY AND MOVE TO MESSINA.

THREE days later we sailed across, landing at Syracuse. Apart from small areas round the docks this town showed very few scars of war. Gangs of Italian prisoners were busy unloading material of all sorts. Convoys of trucks and reinforcements were forming up and moving off into the interior.

Movement control could give us little information of where our units were. I was in charge of several shiploads of vehicles and men, and decided to park for the night outside the town. We spent the evening in a café listening to a very good little band, which from time to time tried valiantly, though not very successfully, to play British tunes, but when they were playing their own native tunes they were excellent. We stayed to the very end, and then continued the party in our own camp till almost dawn.

I had given orders earlier in the evening to start at dawn, and when I was wakened after only one hour's sleep I sincerely regretted my earlier enthusiasm. We moved off in a convoy which stretched out over three miles. I went ahead in a jeep. I had procured some maps, but apart from the information that the division was somewhere beyond Catania, I had no idea where to look or what route to take. Several times we had to make long detours to avoid blown-up bridges, and in spite of an early start it was well on in the evening before we came across the first signs of our own division.

There had been one or two control points on the way, but the situation at the front was changing so rapidly that they could not keep up with it. I was finally directed to go to a town called Paterno (not to be mixed up with the capital Palermo), but when within a few miles of it I learnt by sheer chance from a soldier from whom I was inquiring the way that this town was still in German hands. I found Brigade H.Q. more by luck than good guidance just as it was growing dark. I had to suffer many sarcastic remarks that night—" Are you sure you can spare the time to visit us ? " " By jove ! the Transport Officer believes in playing safe." " Who told you the fighting was finished ? " Later some wag made up a song about " B " echelon arriving the day that Messina, the last German stronghold in Sicily, fell. This was not quite accurate. We arrived six days before ! I also heard the full story of the battle of Gerbini and how many officers had been knocked out. The new commanding officer had asked for me back, and the next day I went up to the battalion. They were resting in a small village on the slopes of Mount Etna not far from Paterno, which had fallen the previous day. When I walked into the Mess there was not a single officer in it whom I knew. It might have been another Mess altogether, and for a second I thought I had made a mistake. I took over a company which was little more than half-strength, and many of these were newly arrived reinforcements.

The night after I arrived there was a group conference, and we were warned to be ready to move by mule transport the following day. I spent the night trying to divide the company stores into loads equivalent to the number of mules which had been allotted to the company, and invariably found the answer coming to fractions of mules. If for no one else's, I was glad for the mule's sake that that move was cancelled. The mule wasn't born that could have taken the loads which it would have been necessary to put on them. We remained another four days in that village, and then learnt that Messina had fallen and, apart from small groups in the mountains, Sicily was clear of Germans.

I was revelling in being back in the battalion, and threw myself with new enthusiasm into building up the company. Except my second-in-command, who was on battalion duty anyway, all the officers were new reinforcements with little or no battle experience, but they were a very good crowd and worked hard. I missed the intimate contact I had been used to with the old company officers, and after the first two days I had to ask them to stop calling me " Sir " in the Mess and jumping up when I came in. We were organised in company Messes, and mine was in quite a pleasant little Italian house with the usual wide verandah. I decided that we needed a real good rousing company officers' dinner and sing-song in order to break the ice. Fortunately the N.A.A.F.I. rations had just arrived, and I had also managed to scrounge an odd bottle of whisky and gin while I was in Africa. I invited the quartermaster, transport officer, and the doctor, about the only old stagers left. The doctor was a born comedian, with an endless repertoire of comic songs. The quartermaster was also a great help in making an evening go with a swing; while the M.T. officer, who only knew two notes in the musical scale and seldom could stay on either, could usually be persuaded to sing, or intone, " Down by the old Millstream," provided one could get him sufficiently mellowed by a well-served dinner with accessories.

My new officers were not too keen on the dinner at first and were a bit inclined to want to excuse themselves, but my plan succeeded beyond all expectations. The M.T. officer and doctor had started celebrating at tea-time, and were already in cracking form by the time they arrived. I had spent great pains on the preparation for the dinner, and the effect was worth it. The M.T. officer was positively benign after the second course, and before the coffee arrived he was already on his feet, without the usual persuasion, rendering his soulful but unmusical version of the sentimental ditty mentioned. The doctor was already imitating Dave Willis, while the quartermaster was violently cursing the company for being the slovenliest and worst disciplined in the battalion, a sure sign that he was all for it. Before they realised it I had the new officers giving a turn, and they rallied round magnificently, and I discovered with growing pleasure that I had a galaxy of talent in the company. All formality was dropped, and Christian names were exchanged quite naturally. The party continued till the early hours of the morning, and we all finally parted completely happy.

It was late that night when we heard the news of the fall of Messina, and this good news added to the general cheerful atmosphere.

The following morning we moved off in convoy bound for the coast a few miles from Messina. It was an interesting and exciting journey. We passed through many villages, most of which bore the scars of battle. The villagers turned out in their hundreds cheering and shouting. Girls leaned over verandahs pouring hundreds of hazel-nuts on to the passing trucks. The Jocks had to pull on their steel helmets to protect themselves. Small children ran alongside the trucks screaming " Caramello ! Caramello ! " (sweets), and the few Jocks who had any threw them out to them. These people, whose homes we had been bombing and shelling and whose fathers and husbands and sons we had been fighting and killing, showed far more genuine friendliness towards us than the French in Tunisia had ever done.

This spontaneous welcome made Mussolini's hysterical messages and slogans, which were painted on every available wall, seem more incongruous than ever. " Obedire ! Credere ! Combattere ! Vinceremo !—Mussolini." ("Obey! Believe! Fight! We shall conquer.") How pathetic these flamboyant slogans looked on the battered walls and balconies from which the people thus exhorted were now welcoming their enemies with the only gifts they had to give. Food and clothing had been destroyed or stolen by the retreating Germans, their money was valueless, their menfolk killed or missing, in many cases their poor houses destroyed, yet they gave us what was to be their only food for many days to come, nuts and wine grapes.

We camped the night by a partially destroyed silk hosiery factory, and many parcels of salvaged silk stockings were to find their way to grateful wives, sweethearts, and sisters in many homes in Central Scotland.

The next day we drove along the coast road to Messina over hastily improvised bridges and bumped across dried-up river-beds. Burnt-out German tanks lay alongside the road; we passed road-blocks partially destroyed with anti-tank guns still in position and dead Germans lying around them. Once we passed a German army car park where vehicles of all descriptions were packed in orderly lines.

As we approached Messina the villages became more deserted and many more destroyed buildings were in evidence. We branched off the main road and cut inland, climbing higher and higher up a mountain-pass on a secondary road which was little more than a cart-track. Some of the trucks stuck, and there were long delays while they were pulled off the narrow road or towed up. Most of them were battle-weary; they had bumped and scraped over thousands of miles of desert and then been disgorged on to shingly beaches from swaying landing-ships, and now this last precipitous climb up the sheer face of a mountain was the last straw.

Our destination was a high headland overlooking the Messina straits. As we approached it, it was already growing dark and we could see a huge red glow of a vast fire burning. The Italians had had a large arsenal in a fort and its surroundings, and part of this had been set on fire before they left; now the whole mountain-side was blazing. We could see the mainland of Italy quite clearly across the straits, which were barely two miles wide, and we could even see German trucks moving along the coastal roads.

We had a long halt just outside our battalion area. With the instinct born of long experience in desert moves, my quartermaster sergeant got the cookers out and started brewing up the evening meal. The Intelligence officer, newly out from England (our original one had been among the wounded at Gerbini) came hurrying across and angrily ordered my cooks to put the fire out because of the black-out. We all burst out laughing and he looked angrily around. I don't think he ever saw the joke. There, just behind us, a whole mountain-side was blazing and he was afraid the Germans would see the pale-blue flicker from our petrol-burners!

We finally moved into our company area and settled

for the night. Everyone expected that we should be attacking the mainland in a day or two and we were determined to get as much sleep as possible, but the next morning we learnt that there would be no early move and my company was detailed for detachment to take over an area some six miles away.

I set off with the battalion second-in-command in a jeep to reconnoitre the area; we went over an even more fantastic mountain-track than the one we had come over the previous night. The track was barely the width of a car and wound round the mountain-side, in twists and turns which made the Blackpool " figure of eight " seem as if it were as straight as a German autobahn. On one side was the precipitous mountain-side, and on the other, unguarded by any fence or even curb, a sheer drop of sixty to three hundred feet. As we gingerly nosed our way round one particularly fantastic turn, a jeep came rocking round the opposite corner. A crash was inevitable, and unfortunately we were on the " sheer drop " side. I was in the back and I instinctively prepared to dive out on to the road. Our driver desperately tried to squeeze closer to the edge in the hope that there would be sufficient room to allow the oncoming jeep to pass, but there wasn't a hope. It caught us a glancing blow as it skidded up to us with brakes screeching. For one second our jeep swayed on the edge. I had flung myself over to the roadside, and I think my weight saved us. It righted itself and remained precariously balanced with the front wheel over the edge. The driver gingerly backed on to the road again and we all scrambled out shakily. I peeped over the edge and, as if to rub in the fate we had so narrowly missed, I saw far below the tangled remains of an Italian truck which had recently gone over. Then the second-in-command and I turned furiously on the white-faced young officer who was coming towards us, having pulled his jeep out of the bank opposite. In the same instant we started to curse him, and if ever an officer heard a candid opinion of his mentality, appearance, birth, and future prospects, that chap did. He was almost more shaken than we were, and after his hundredth apology, when he climbed back into his jeep to continue the journey, he moved off as if in a funeral column. We also continued our journey, but we were too shaken to talk at first; somehow it seemed a worse experience than any we had had in battle.

That afternoon I moved off from Battalion H.Q. in my 15-cwt. truck with the company following behind. It had been difficult enough to negotiate that road in a jeep, but leading a convoy of 3-tonners was a positive nightmare, and when I finally arrived with my company intact I breathed a prayer of thanksgiving. I was to travel that road many times during the next two weeks to attend conferences at Battalion H.Q., but I never lost the feeling of terror with which I started each journey. The alternative route via the coast was in full view of the enemy and was therefore forbidden during the early days, but in spite of that I preferred it and used it whenever possible, gladly risking the double danger of being shot up by the enemy and " rocketed " by the commanding officer.

## CHAPTER XXIII.

### PROBLEMS OF OCCUPATION.

I SHALL always look back upon the month that followed as one of the happiest times I spent in the Army. The ice had been completely broken by that cheery party we had had before leaving Paterno, and no company commander could have wished for better companions than the officers whom I now commanded. As individuals they could not have differed more in character, appearance, and personality, and yet together they made up a first-class company team both in their original capacities within the company and off duty in the Mess. The commanding officer, having satisfied himself that all was going well in the visits he paid us during the first few days, then left us almost entirely on our own. The only contact we had with the rest of the battalion was the periodical visits I made to Battalion H.Q. for routine conferences.

Our duties were manifold and interesting and we had little opportunity for training, but with the able help and enthusiasm of my officers I was able to build up a really live company team from the various elements which made up the personnel. We had about thirty old stagers, including a real war-horse of a company sergeant-major; a further thirty with a little battle experience gained in almost every theatre of war; the rest were completely battle innocent.

The only snag that arose to hinder us was the appalling epidemic of malaria which swept through the battalion at this time. My company suffered with the rest, and at one time I had 35 per cent of my total personnel down with it. Fortunately in most cases it was not a serious type, though we had one death and three or four on the danger list, and I lost my company sergeant-major at a time when his influence was most required to weld the company together.

All the officers except myself took it at one time or another, though they were only off for short periods.

The camp was situated in a vineyard and olive-grove about a half-mile from the main coast. Our duties consisted of patrolling the coastal area, with the main object of preventing escapes to the mainland by the many German and Italian soldiers still wandering in the hills. We had Bren guns posted at various points on the coast, and when we saw boats pushing off under cover of darkness we would fire a warning burst at them, and then, if they continued, we would pour magazine after magazine into them. In spite of our vigilance, however, there was a good deal of traffic over the straits at this period. We also had observation posts, from which we watched German troop movements across the straits. We used to send out patrols into the hills to try and round up odd groups of Germans whose presence had been reported to us by the local villagers.

At first discipline in the occupied area was very slack. A.M.G.O.T., the organisation semi-military, semi-civilian, for administrating occupied territory, was nominally in charge of the area, but this organisation made little or no attempt to administrate anywhere, and only succeeded in destroying the goodwill which the Jocks had built up between themselves and the local inhabitants.

Messina was a shambles. Never have I seen a town so completely destroyed. The R.A.F. and American Air Force had bombed it into dust, and then the Germans had completed the destruction by shelling from the mainland. The inhabitants had taken to the hills and small villages around. Bands of starving children wandered about among the ruins, and came and pressed their noses against the barbed-wire entanglements we had to build round the camps to keep them out. They were pitiful sights, many too young to realise what had happened to them. Parents and homes had disappeared and they were fast becoming savages. Our troops, although themselves on short rations, shared their meals with them, but it was often dangerous to wander too far from the camp after night except in groups, for some of these child gangs were adepts with the knife. Along the roads poured a continuous stream of refugees, including many hundreds of Italian and Sicilian soldiers. Many of these begged us to take them into custody, but we had to refuse, for we had no supplies for them. The roads were congested, and military convoys were held up by hundreds of donkey-carts piled high with salvaged household goods.

If any attempt was made by A.M.G.O.T. to control this refugee problem, or even to administrate the area, it was a very feeble one and a complete failure, and everywhere detachments like my own were unofficially trying to take on the job and reduce the chaos to some sort of order. Soon my company office became a kind of county control office combined with a local magistrates' court. With the help of a Latin dictionary unearthed in a bomb-shattered school and a small boy called Tony who had learnt a little English at school, I governed and administered the area, doling out rough justice and mediating between rival claimants for salvaged goods, &c.

The justice was very rough. For example, two excited Italians came before me one morning, both claiming to be the owner of a bicycle. They cursed and screamed at each other, and showed such complete " contempt of court " that, after failing to extract proof of ownership from either of them, I ruled that the cycle be confiscated. This decision, after the first shock, seemed to please both; for each was so delighted that the other had not succeeded in getting it. The cycle was used by the Company H.Q. personnel for taking messages to outposts.

To add to the confusion the authorities proclaimed a curfew, by which everyone was to be in their houses by 8 P.M. As more than 50 per cent of the population had no houses to be in, this caused a wave of unnecessary arrests, with all the resultant herding of large numbers into cages, from which they had to be hastily released when it was finally realised by the authorities that, having arrested them, we were responsible for feeding them.

My heart sank when I received an order from Brigade to round up all enemy ex-soldiers. I hastily pointed out that this would include hundreds of local villagers who had been in the " Home Guard " on beach defences and who had since returned to their farms, where they were of much more assistance to us than as prisoners whom we would have to feed. This objection was overruled in the airy way such objections are, by people who are not in touch with the situation. With great reluctance I gave the order, and within six hours the small cage I had made from scraps of wire lying about was packed out, and Italians of all descriptions were overflowing into the camp. It was impossible to attempt to guard such numbers even if they required it, but as 90 per cent were voluntary prisoners who were only too glad to shift the responsibility of feeding themselves into other hands, there was little need to guard anything except our cookhouse. When I had asked what arrangements were to be made about feeding them, I had been told to indent for food supplies through the usual channel. Of course when I sent in an indent to the quartermaster for a further 600 rations he went off the deep-end, and naturally couldn't and wouldn't supply them. I hastily carted the prisoners off, packed like sardines into my only two trucks, and soon cries of consternation came back from Brigade, where preparations had been made for a few dozen prisoners only. The wretched prisoners were returned to me in droves, and having no alternative I released them again.

These incidents are amusing to look back upon, but were infuriating at the time. For the next few days our lives were pestered by continual streams of dirty, half-starving Italian soldiers, to whom the news had been spread that we were " taking in prisoners." Finally we had to put up a large notice, " No prisoners taken here." After a few days, too, numbers of anxious women, relatives of the men who had not been returned, came begging for information, and we then learnt that some of the men who had given themselves up as soldiers had never been soldiers at all, but had done so in the hope of getting a square meal. The food situation was going from bad to worse. An announcement had been made apparently by A.M.G.O.T. to the civilian population that food supplies would follow the armies, but if this announcement was made there were certainly no food supplies in the area I was in.

It is difficult to make a balanced judgment of where the responsibility lay, but later, when I visited the American zone, I could not help noticing the comparison— a comparison which was most unfavourable to the British administration. First, it was obvious that we had not been prepared for such a complete clean-up of all foodstuff by the Germans; secondly, one had to bear in mind, when feeling inclined to sympathise with these wretched people, that they had been our enemies, and as such ready to sneak into a war which was no concern of theirs for the sake of accepting any loot left over by the Germans, and it was therefore their own fault when their German friends and masters finally grabbed all their own possessions. They had accepted and acclaimed Mussolini's war when it appeared to offer them a cheap way of looting the "beaten" British, and in the countries they had occupied, by kind permission of their German masters, they had outdone the Germans in their ruthless exploitation and pillaging; but from a purely practical standpoint this state of affairs should, and could, have been avoided.

Whereas the American organisation for administration was a carefully prepared one, with personnel who spoke the language and had had experience of civil administration, ours was a last-minute makeshift with a large proportion of the personnel chosen on the spot, and it was in the choosing of the personnel that we fell down so badly. An area would be occupied, and it would then be realised that we required a town major. "Requests" would be sent out to local units, and, tracing it down to the ultimate stage, a "demand" would be received by the adjutant to supply one officer, preferably with experience, for duties as town major. Not unnaturally the commanding officer would send the man he least minded losing, and therefore in nine cases out of ten the man least suitable for such a responsible job. This man usually had neither the ability, character, or even inclination for the job. To make matters worse he would arrive to find that all the local officials had been sacked because they were Fascists. But after twenty years of Fascism there was no one but Fascists left who were capable of civil administration; for only those who were good Fascists had been allowed to receive the necessary training. So the original officials would have to be reinstated; they would then promptly start making things as difficult as possible, and would organise black markets and engage in every kind of graft. The local police were of no assistance; they were unbelievably idle, and certainly would not expose a Fascist official. The language difficulty, a problem at any time, would be used as an excuse for ignoring or disobeying orders received from the A.M.G.O.T. official. Meanwhile the anti-Fascist section of the population, who had shown themselves in the open on the arrival of the British, would now be persecuted by officials and police, and not unnaturally became very bitter towards the British Occupying Authorities. Known Fascists could be seen running about everywhere in their private cars with an A.M.G.O.T. official pass on their windscreen. They blatantly used their cars for private purposes at a time when we were forbidden to use our trucks for even army purposes, owing to the necessity to conserve petrol. These officials appeared to have limitless petrol supplies.

All this was avoided by the Americans, because they had made adequate preparations, but it must be remembered that the Americans' problems were far simpler than ours. First, they had an enormous American Italian population to draw on, thus overcoming the language problem; secondly, all the real hard fighting had been in the British zone, and Palermo, the capital and centre of the American zone, was almost untouched, while Messina, and to a lesser extent Catania, were completely devastated; thirdly, their people were not half as fully engaged in the war as we were, and at that time had been for four years. But we were too slow to learn the lesson; for we heard of many more examples of bad organisation before we left. I believe and sincerely hope, not only for the sake of the other nations we have freed, but also for our own soldiers' sake, that the lesson has been learnt now.

## CHAPTER XXIV.

### THE LIGHTER SIDE OF LIFE ON DETACHMENT.

LIFE was by no means all serious during this time; in spite of our manifold duties we had quite a lot of spare time. We used to bathe almost daily; the sea was beautifully warm and calm, and we would sun-bathe afterwards until dark. Often in the evenings we had sing-songs, and the boys used to invite an Italian family who lived opposite us to join in. Whatever defects the Italians had, they could sing, and we would all ask over and over again for " La Donna è mobile " and other Italian songs. One girl of about fifteen years sang " Ave Maria " beautifully, and in that setting, with the wind gently rustling the vines and the moon gleaming on the Mediterranean, a strange hush would spread over the crowd of rough soldiers, who a moment before had been yelling some bawdy song at the top of their voices. These Italians enjoyed the evenings as much as we did, and sometimes they used to bring friends who could play the mandolin.

As autumn approached we moved to a nearby location where there was a little house with a veranda overlooking the sea. We scrounged a piano and an oil lamp, and used to have dinners to which we invited other officers.

One of my officers was a born scrounger. I first discovered this by asking him to try and get some real eating grapes, for we had the commanding officer coming for dinner, and wanted to offer something better than the little wine-grapes which grew all around us. He returned an hour later with a whole donkey-cart complete with three enormous baskets. After I had got over my surprise he produced some bottles of really good liqueurs. After that he became organiser-in-chief of all festivities, and he never once let us down. Once he produced sufficient beer for the whole company, apparently having beaten the N.A.A.F.I. by a short head to possession of a disused brewery. I overlooked the fact that he had no right to have been in that area and had taken my truck without permission.

On another occasion my second-in-command and I were invited to a lunch by an Italian family in the adjoining village. I had befriended the little boy, who was a cheery little chap of ten years. He had been teaching me Italian, and in the process we had become fast friends. His father had fought with the British in the last war and had been wounded. It was pathetic how hard they tried to give us a real good meal. We had *hors d'œuvre* from their own garden produce, veal and spaghetti (it was a mystery where the veal came from), tomatoes, rice, and local cheese. He had a good wine-cellar, and we had brought along a bottle of whisky, which we had presented to him. He served it neat, as a liqueur, in beautiful crystal liqueur glasses. Soon the inevitable party of neighbours began to gather, bringing their mandolins and infant prodigies. Everybody sang, and the children danced for us. Most of the tunes were familiar by this time, and as our host furnished us with song-sheets we were enabled to join in. The party, which had started at 1 P.M., lasted far into the evening, and then, in spite of the pouring rain, for there had been a thunderstorm, our host and his two eldest sons insisted on escorting us the whole way back to our Mess. When we got back we found that the others in our absence had started a party of their own, so we all joined in and sang and celebrated till far into the night.

During the first round-up of prisoners we had kept two for duties in the cook-house. This was quite illegal, and originally I had intended to send them off as soon as some of my own men returned from hospital, where they were recovering from malaria. However, we had become so attached to these two, whom we called Mussolini and Ciano, that we hung on to them. One day when I was holding a scale A inspection of the company I found these two dressed up in khaki-drill and balmorals on parade with the rest of the company. We were just preparing to move into Italy, and they asked if they could come and fight with us as far as their home in Naples. Actually we were only over on the mainland for three days while we furnished the " firm base " from which the Canadians launched their first attack, and I left the two Italians with " B " echelon. They were very hurt when I told them what I was going to do, but when we returned they pranced round me like a couple of spaniels.

The following day we heard that Italy had surrendered unconditionally. All the village people sat on their balconies throughout that night singing and shouting. They thought that all their troubles were over, and now that Badoglio had asked for peace everything would return to normal. Actually it made no difference at all to us or them. Food supplies were beginning to trickle through now and the roads were gradually clearing of refugees, though for weeks longer there were continual streams of released Sicilian soldiers trudging wearily home. (The Sicilians were released at once, but the Italians were held for further arrangements.)

The autumn rains were beginning to set in and we moved once more, this time to a barracks by the seashore. Again we were lucky enough to get a little house for a company Mess, though this time we had to share it with the officers of another company and its real owners. These people were out-and-out Fascists and showed clearly their resentment of our presence. They had been allotted the kitchen and two bedrooms for their own use, but they insisted on coming into the room we were using as our Mess and sitting chattering there. We ordered them out, at first politely and latterly very abruptly, but they always returned. We held one or two parties here; there was a nearby family consisting of father, mother, and three girls in their late teens. These three girls were a great attraction to the younger officers, but father was very strict and would not let them out of his sight. **One** of them sang and played the piano beautifully, and we used to visit their home or invite them to our Mess and sit for hours listening to vocal and piano solos.

Now that the necessity for patrolling and mopping up was finished we were back to ordinary training during the day, but most of our evenings were free. We used to go a three-mile run early every morning, finishing up with a plunge in the sea, which at that hour had quite a nip. Then we would train till 4.30 P.M., after which, except for officers' training on certain nights, we were free. During this time leave was granted; it was the first leave most of us had had since we came out in June 1942, though those of us who had been wounded had had convalescent leave. The leave was arranged by companies, a whole company going off at one time. We had only four and a half days, but my officers and I agreed to go to Palermo, about 160 miles away on the other side of the island. We were granted the use of the company 15-cwt. truck, and having stocked it with four days' rations we set off.

## CHAPTER XXV.

### LEAVE IN PALERMO.

I HAVE already remarked that although we got on so well together we were a very mixed crowd. My second-in-command was a young but very efficient and battle-experienced officer who had joined the battalion with the first batch of reinforcements during the battle of Alamein. He had a keen sense of humour and a great zest for life.

Of the three subalterns, one, the perfect scrounger, was over thirty years, married, with three children. He had been out as long as me but in another battalion of the same regiment. He was tough, full to overflowing with self-confidence, loud-voiced, argumentative, and a rabid Scottish Nationalist. He hated and despised all foreigners, and particularly Arabs and Italians, whom he treated the same, even to addressing the Italians in Arabic slang, but all hatred for foreigners was subordinated to his fanatical dislike of the English "oppressors" of his beloved Scotland. He had unbounded faith in the Jock as a fighter, but thought the English were better confined to the more menial tasks in the rear. Once, when a well-meaning Italian had shouted a welcome to the "Inglese" soldiers, he had stopped his platoon truck and, leaping out, had nearly shaken the life out of the terrified wretch, while trying to make him understand that he was Scotsezi, something on a grade so infinitely highly removed from the Inglesi species as not to be classed together even among the white nations. This fanaticism gave us endless cause for enjoyment, and I am afraid I shamelessly exploited his feelings by leading the conversation into dangerous channels whenever things were dull in the Mess.

The next subaltern was the extreme opposite. Scots on one side of his family, but born and brought up in England, he was completely English in his ways and outlook. A typical product of an English public school and Oxford. He was a regular soldier, twice as efficient as the Scots Nationalist, but he lacked confidence in himself and was the unluckiest man I have ever met for " landing rockets." Well-read and extremely cultured, he was as international in his outlook (for he had lived several years on the Continent) as the Scottish Nationalist was bigoted. Over-serious, he opened himself to ragging, but, especially where the Scottish Nationalist was concerned, he could hold his own and tear the latter's theories to pieces in fierce arguments. Both were excellent platoon commanders, but while the rough-and-ready, " don't care a damn," " all for your Jocks " Scottish Nationalist was understood and appreciated by the men, the methodical, conscientious, rather worried actions of the " regular soldier " were treated with suspicion, which his " English tongue " did nothing to relieve. Both these officers were grand fun in a party, and the regular had an endless repertoire of songs which he could put over with a zest which kept us in fits of laughter when his natural diffidence had been washed away in alcohol.

The third subaltern was very young; twenty-one, I think; quiet, slow, loyal, but lazy. Unlike the rest of us who were all fairly hard drinkers, he was a complete abstainer, an arrangement which, though it must have tried him on many occasions, we, after our first surprise, found of considerable advantage. He made up for a lack of willingness or ability to sing by playing the piano, thus completing the necessary functions for a satisfactory Mess. He was as kind and good-natured to the Italians as the Scottish Nationalist was rough, and in his quiet unhurrying way he looked after his men and won their trust, a process which was speeded up by his quiet but pronounced Glasgow accent.

This was the crowd, therefore, that set off with me late that September 1943 to spend a holiday together in Palermo. We took my driver and his friend along with us, and we officers sat in the back of the truck singing and shouting back to the people who greeted us as we raced through the coastal villages. There were still many signs of the recent fighting, but as we approached the American zone we saw less and less damage, for the Germans had concentrated in the east of the island and the Americans had had an almost unopposed advance until they arrived at the outskirts of Messina. They had come along the coast road from the west, while we were fighting our way up along the east coast. It was a beautiful run and one well worth covering again under peace conditions. Having made a late start we failed to reach Palermo that night and spent the night camping by the roadside. The following morning we drove into the town.

We were delighted to find it almost intact, with shops and cinemas open, though the former were rather misleading; for they had little to offer except for the inevitable trinkets and souvenirs. We went to the American Army Billeting Officer and inquired about accommodation. He told us that all the hotels had been taken over by the American Army, but after a little hesitation he fixed us up in a very nice one which had been requisitioned as a rest-house for American officers. He also fixed up our driver and his friend in comfortable digs.

After unpacking our kit we strolled into the bar, wondering what sort of reception we should get from the American officers. We were wearing the kilt and this caused a great sensation. We were immediately invited into the group round the bar and were stood drinks without limit. Many of those present had never seen a kilt before except in pictures or on the stage, and they couldn't get over it. More than half of them claimed Scottish ancestors. There was one captain, a real Southerner with a drawl that was almost incomprehensible, who appointed himself our special guardian and host. He arranged for a late drinking pass for us and advised us how to spend our time. He had an appointment twenty miles away at 2 P.M., but at 3 P.M. he was still with us. I hoped he would not get into trouble.

After he left we strolled out into the street and then separated. We had all been advised to go and see " the stiffs." This had completely puzzled us until we were told that it meant the famous catacombs in which the good citizens of Palermo had been mummified and placed on shelves in the walls for generations, until it was stopped by the Italian government in the 1880's. We went there in a gharry, the driver of which was much more anxious to show us live senoritas than long-dead bodies.

At the entrance to the catacombs was a monk sitting at a small pay-desk. He looked doubtfully at our British military currency notes and turned to a small smartly dressed boy, who asked us in broken English how much they were worth in dollars. A crowd quickly gathered round us, staring and whispering excitedly while pointing to our kilts. The small boy asked if we were Cossacks, and seemed disappointed when we told him we were Scotsezi. He seemed to know vaguely where that was, but the others looked blankly at us and asked us in turn whether we were Russians, Greeks, Albanians, or French, pointing excitedly to a large ancient map of Europe. When we pointed to Scotland they all chorused " Inglesi," and I had to restrain the Scottish Nationalist from attacking them.

We went round the catacombs with our small boy as guide, jabbering away in a mixture of English and Italian, and, when he got excited, breaking into German. I spoke to him in German and he replied fluently, telling me that he had learnt it first at school and then for the last three years he had been showing German soldiers round. He showed us the visitors' book with page after page of German names, and then abruptly American names and addresses started. The Scottish Nationalist signed his name with a big flourish, underlining Scotland heavily.

There was really not much to see in the catacombs, although the corpses were detailed off in caves marked Virgins, Bishops, Doctors, &c. A virgin " mummy " looked very much the same as an ancient town councillor. The preserving process was very primitive. The bodies, with entrails removed, were left to dry in the sun on a broad stone slab, and were then dressed and placed in niches in the walls.  Some of the wealthier ones were in elaborate coffins with glass lids, but the majority were just pushed up on the shelves.  I asked how the custom had started, and was informed that a celebrated Palermo explorer had visited Egypt and had been so impressed with the Egyptian mummies that he had returned to introduce the custom to his own town.  Personally I found these dried-up shrivelled corpses reminded me too much of sights I had seen in the desert, where the hot sun and the sand had caused the same process.

We visited the cathedral and the palace, the latter showing clear signs of recent German occupation, and then we strolled into a restaurant.  We were immediately pounced on by four American N.C.O.s, who insisted on standing us more drinks.  Soon we were involved in a furious political debate.  The great difference between the British and the American soldier I found was that, while the former (officers included) were usually bored stiff with politics and the why's and wherefore's of the war, of which they were appallingly ignorant, the American soldier is intensely interested in both.  I enjoyed that debate immensely; the Americans hit out and did not attempt to spare feelings, but they took hard knocks too without showing any resentment.  They blamed us violently for Munich and accused us of being " fight shy " in France.  With all their intense interest they were shockingly ignorant of Britain generally and the Empire in particular.  The usual accusation that we forced the unwilling " colonial " soldiers to fight our battles for us came out early, followed by the extraordinary statement that America had had to pull the chestnuts out of the fire for us again and had had to come and save the situation in Africa, when we were completely licked.  They said our people generally were snobbish and unfriendly, and our officers in particular.

We gave as good as we got; they had no answer when I pointed out that the Germans would never have dared to start the war if the Americans had not shirked their world responsibilities between the wars, and in particular in 1938. I reminded them that America had depended on the British Navy to protect their Atlantic seaboard, that we had held out for over a year all alone without a proper army. I pointed out that we had already beaten Rommel before the Americans landed in Africa, and that even after they landed very few of them did any fighting, and those who did had not been conspicuously successful and had had to be helped out by our own First Army, which had already got enough on its hands at the time; that if we had been green in France, they were greener in Africa, in spite of their vastly superior equipment. I admitted that we had had to depend on their equipment, but reminded them that we were fighting their war with it for over two years before they finally joined us, and even then they had allowed themselves to be caught out at Pearl Harbour.

The harder I hit them the more they showed their appreciation, and when we finally broke up (because the bar had closed) they all shook hands warmly and invited us to their Mess to meet the other fellows; for, as one said, " You sure have given us something to think about, although I still think you are a lot of b—— snobs and you were yellow in France," and another added, " I guess if the big noises back home would get down to it like us and stop all this back-scratching, we would soon get to understand each other and really get together."

We met them again the next day, and for sheer hospitality and good-fellowship one could not have found a better crowd anywhere. This time we were initiated into the mysteries of the Confederate *versus* Yankees, and all except the " Regular " promptly voted for the South.

The next evening we had an uproarious party in a big hotel in the suburbs. We ate an enormous quantity of omelettes, which was all that was on the menu, and later on we sang American and Scottish songs. There were about fifteen of us, representing all three Services of both the British and American Forces, and it was the best get-together that could have been devised. We certainly obeyed the instructions we had all received some time previously to do all in our power to establish friendly relations with our American counterparts. But this was no artificially organised meeting for the furtherance of friendly relations between the Allies. This was a spontaneous gathering with real friendship, based on mutual respect and knowledge of each other's failings. It was a respect born of straight talking, with no attempt at sugaring, and because of that it succeeded where so many well-intentioned efforts preceded by flowery speeches of praise had failed. The American appreciates frank speaking, and the blunter it is the better. That is what they are used to and what they miss most in our honest but misguided attempts to act as perfect hosts at home.

I was to go to one of these well-intentioned efforts when I returned home, where I heard a specially picked officer tell at a representative gathering of Americans how grateful we were for the way they had saved us from disaster and how everything we had been able to do was due to their help. That speech must have done terrible harm to the cause it was attempting to further, and it was all I could do to sit through it.

We were very reluctant to leave Palermo, where we had enjoyed American hospitality at its best, and the parting act of kindness left a lasting impression. The American authorities at the hotel refused to accept a penny in payment, and we had lived there like lords for four days!

We returned to find the battalion seething with excitement. We were going home.

A week or so later we were on our way to Britain.

# EPILOGUE

Hugh Samwell recounts the actions and events in which he was engaged with refreshing simplicity in the pages of this fascinating memoir. What makes his story so different from the many that have been published over the years is that it was written as it happened, not at some later date when it could be embellished with the received words from other stories and the knowledge of the historians. We know this for sure because Hugh Samwell did not live to see the end of the war. He was killed in action on 13 January 1945.

*

The 51st (Highland) Division finally returned to the United Kingdom in November 1943. By this stage, Samwell had been decorated for his actions in North Africa. In a supplement to *The London Gazette* of 4 May 1943, the War Office announced that "the King has been graciously pleased to approve the following awards in recognition of gallant and distinguished services in the Middle East". On the list was "Lieutenant (acting Captain) Hugh de Lancy Samwell (73830), The Argyll and Sutherland Highlanders (Princess Louise's) (Stirling)", who was awarded the Military Cross for his actions during the fighting on the Mareth Line in March 1943.

Prior to returning to the UK, Samwell had been involved in defending soldiers accused of mutiny in September 1943. The men, predominantly from the 50th (Northumbrian) and 51st (Highland) divisions, had been part of a number that sailed from Tripoli believing that they were en route to join the rest of their units which were then based in Sicily. Once aboard ship, they were, however, informed that they were to be taken to Salerno to reinforce the 46th Division.

The situation was exacerbated by a lack of organisation when the men reached Salerno, leaving them angry and frustrated. Most of the soldiers, a thousand or so fresh recruits, were reallocated to their new units, leaving a group of 500 men who were mostly veterans of the fighting in North Africa. By 20 September the situation remained little changed, the men still refusing postings to unfamiliar units. They were addressed by the commander of X Corps who admitted that a mistake had been made, and promised that they would rejoin their old units once Salerno was secure. The men were also warned of the consequences of mutiny in wartime.

Of the three hundred in the field, 108 decided to follow orders, leaving a hard core of 192. They were all charged with mutiny under the Army Act – reputedly the largest number of men accused at any one time in British military history.

The accused were shipped to Algeria, where the proceedings opened towards the end of October. All were found guilty, and three sergeants were sentenced to death. The sentences were subsequently commuted to twelve years forced labour and eventually suspended.

Having returned to the UK in 1943, after a period of leave the 7th Battalion The Argyll and Sutherland Highlanders settled down to training in preparation for the forthcoming D-Day landings. In March, it moved to East Anglia and on 5 April 1944, transferred from XXX Corps to I Corps and commenced training for the Normandy landings. In June, the division moved to the River Thames and embarked. The 154th Brigade still comprised the 1st and 7th Black Watch and 7th Argylls.

The 51st (Highland) Division went ashore to the west of the Ornnemouth in I Corps' area and soon crossed the River Orne. The fighting in the following weeks was some of the worst the division had experienced so far in the war.

In the months that followed, the Highlanders fought their way across France and into Holland. Whilst the British were preparing the break out across the Rhine into Germany, Hitler unleashed his great counter-attack through the Ardennes in the last days of 1944. The 51st (Highland) Division along with the 53rd (Welsh) Division and the 43rd (Wessex) Division, plus three armoured brigades, were given the immediate task of securing the Meuse crossing between Namur and Liège.

The German counter-attack was halted and the Allied forces returned to the offensive. In bitterly cold weather and through deep snow, the Highlanders launched their attack on 7 January 1945. As the days wore on, the troops liberated the villages of Hodister, Wairzy, Cheoux, Genes, Halleux, Rochampy and Lignière.

On the morning of 11 January the Highland Division, preceded by armoured reconnaissance units of the 2nd Derbyshire Regiment and tanks of the 1st Northamptonshire Regiment, crossed the River Ourthe and entered the devastated town of La Roche. Darkness found the men of the 7th Argylls resting on the roadside. The following morning the advance was to continue. The battalion's War Diary provides an insight to the events that day:

"08.00. Bn continued to move forward and debussed outside La Roche. We continued on foot with 'A' Coy leading followed by Bn HQ, 'B' Coy and 'D' Coy. The advance continued through Hives (4574) (now held by 7 BW) then 'A' Coy who were just forward of Hives ran into heavy shelling and M/G fire from a wooded hill on the left which dominated the road. Three or four Panther tanks were spotted and at least one S.P. gun."

In the ensuing fire fight, a number of Highlanders were killed. Amongst them was Hugh Samwell, now an Acting Major, who had been leading his men from the front as always. He was 33-years-old.

*

Samwell was buried in the Commonwealth War Graves Commission Cemetery at Hotton, some thirty miles south-east of Namur, along with forty-one of his comrades. He never saw his book in print.

# INDEX

## FIGHTING WITH THE DESERT RATS

Aldershot, 11, 29

Alexandria, 15, 20, 60, 78, 139

Algeria, 153, 154, 160, 162, 164, 176

Algiers, 58, 163, 171

Allied Military Government for Occupied Territories (A.M.G.O.T.), 192, 193, 195, 196

Amarya Transit Camp, 78, 80

Americans and United States of America, 58, 63, 117, 126, 156, 162, 163, 165, 166, 169, 170, 171, 180, 181, 195, 196, 197, 204, 206, 207, 208

Arnim, Colonel-General Hans-Jügen von, 160

Auchinleck, Field Marshal Sir Claude John Eyre, GCB, GCIE, CSI, DSO, OBE, 58, 88

Australians, 17, 18, 20, 21, 22, 23

Austria, 47

Belgium, 47

Ben Gardane, 143, 147, 148

Benghazi, 44, 79, 80, 81, 83, 86, 90, 92

Bizerta, 160

Boer War, 61

British Army, 28, 77, 80-1, 84, 85, 90, 91, 96, 110, 112, 113, 118, 119, 128, 144, 158, 169, 175, 191

Ist Army, 59

Eighth Army, 22, 37, 86, 135, 149, 154, 160, 165, 167

Brigade Light Aid Detachments (R.E.M.E.), 99

Catering Corps, 114

Royal Army Medical Corps (R.A.M.C.), 138

Royal Army Service Corps (R.A.S.C.), 86, 91, 142, 143, 148

Royal Electrical and Mechanical Engineers

(R.E.M.E.), 99, 176
Royal Engineers, 80
British Broadcasting Corporation (BBC), 37, 180, 182
Bulgaria, 163

Cairo, 15, 17, 55-76, 77, 111, 113, 182
Cape Town, 13
Carthage, 181
Churchill, Sir Winston Leonard Spencer, KG, OM, CH, TD, PC, DL, FRS, 14, 19, 114, 115, 140, 182
Ciano, Galaezzo, Italian Foreign Minister, 199
Commonwealth War Graves Commission, 182
Crete, 175
Cyrenaican-Tripolitanian border, 88

De Gaulle, Charles André Joseph Marie, 164, 171, 173

Egypt, 15, 50, 139, 206

Egyptians, 17, 21
El Agheila, 58, 88
El Alamein Battle of, 22, 28-37, 38-50, 93, 94, 95, 114, 142, 181, 182, 202
El Alamein Railway Station, 23, 24
El Daba, 74
Enfideville (Enfidaville), 154, 155, 156, 158, 162, 182
Entertainments National Service Association (ENSA), 140

France, 47, 82, 153, 163, 164, 165, 172, 173, 174, 175, 206, 207
France Battle of, 28
Franco-Prussian War, 172
Free French Forces, 17, 19, 20, 21, 78, 160
Freetown, Sierra Leone, 13
French Army, 173

Gabes, 144, 146, 150
George VI, King of the United Kingdom, 114
Gerbini, Battle of, 177, 183, 185, 188

German Army, 15, 24, 25, 26, 28, 29, 40, 41, 42, 43, 45, 46, 48, 49, 52, 83, 84, 85, 89, 91, 103, 108, 110, 111, 121, 129, 135, 150, 153, 161, 164, 188, 192
    Afrika Korps, 15, 81, 122
Giraud, General Henri Honoré, 173
Greece, 61, 175

Hitler, Adolf, 130
Homs, 100

India, 61
Italian Forces, 31, 74, 105, 108, 110, 111, 122, 150, 161, 180, 182, 188, 192

Leptis Magna, 100-1
London, 68, 86, 165, 174

Mareth Line, 116, 117, 139, 140, 143, 144, 152, 164, 171
Medenine, 122, 126, 137, 143
Mersah-Matruh Road, 23
Messina, 184, 185, 187, 188, 192, 197, 204
Montgomery, Field Marshal Bernard Law, First Viscount Montgomery of Alamein, KG, GCB, DSO, PC, 13, 19, 144
Morocco, 162, 164
Mosley, Sir Oswald Ernald, 173
Mount Etna, 185
Mussolini, Benito Amilcare Andrea, 21, 79, 80, 82, 83, 88, 100, 187, 199

Naples, 200
Navy, Army and Air Force Institutes, (NAAFI), 79, 88, 127, 143, 147, 148, 149, 186, 199
New York, 144
New Zealand, 50, 53, 144, 156
Nile, 15

Palermo, 184, 197, 202, 204, 205, 206, 208
Palestine, 65, 67, 68, 84, 90
Paterno, 184, 185, 191
Pearl Harbour, 207
Poland, 47

Port Tewfik, 14

Ritchie, General Sir Neil Methuen, GBE, KCB, DSO, MC, KStJ, 19
Rommel, Field Marshal Erwin Johannes Eugen, 15, 16, 20, 22, 28, 55, 88, 117, 121, 126, 136, 154, 171, 172
Royal Air Force, 20, 76, 192
Royal Navy, 20, 113, 171
Sfax, 150, 151, 152, 153, 163, 175
Sicily, 136, 180, 183, 184, 185, 200
Sirte, 86, 91, 92, 93, 109
Smuts, Jan Christiaan, OM, CH, ED, KC, FRS, PC, 54
Sousse, 150, 154, 156, 163
South Africa, 50, 51, 52, 53, 54
Stalin, Joseph Vissarionovich, 114
Suez Canal, 14, 16
Syracuse, 184

Tobruk, 14, 19, 48, 60, 74, 81
Tripoli, 18, 58, 93, 95, 99, 103, 106, 107, 109, 110-115, 116, 117, 134, 135, 137, 139, 144, 152, 169, 182

Tunis, 58, 116, 139, 149, 150, 154, 160, 163, 174, 181, 182
Tunisia, 176, 187
Turkey, 163

United States Air Force, 192

Vichy, 163, 164, 172, 174

Wadi Akarit, 144
Wavell, Field Marshal Archibald Percival First Earl Wavell, GCB, GCSI, GCIE, CMG, MC, PC, 88

Yugoslavia, 61

Zuara, 142

# Tracing Your Family History?

## Read Your Family History

**ESSENTIAL ADVICE FROM THE EXPERTS**

**FREE COPY**

*Your Family History* is the only magazine that is put together by expert genealogists. Our editorial team, led by Dr Nick Barratt, is passionate about family history, and our networks of specialists are here to give essential advice, helping readers to find their ancestors and solve those difficult questions.

In each issue we feature a **Beginner's Guide** covering the basics for those just getting started, a **How To** ... section to help you to dig deeper into your family tree and the opportunity to **Ask The Experts** about your tricky research problems. We also include a **Spotlight** on a different county each month and a **What's On** guide to the best family history courses and events, plus much more.

**Receive a free copy** of *Your Family History* magazine and gain essential advice and all the latest news. To request a free copy of a recent back issue, simply e-mail your name and address to marketing@your-familyhistory.com or call 01226 734302*.

*Your Family History* is in all good newsagents and also available on subscription for six or twelve issues. For more details on how to take out a subscription, call 01778 392013 or visit **www.your-familyhistory.co.uk**.

Alternatively read issue 31 online completely free using this QR code

*Free copy is restricted to one per household and available while stocks last.

## www.your-familyhistory.com